Notes from the

Café

R.F. Georgy

Parthenon Books

New York

R.F. Georgy

Published by Parthenon Books, New York

Paperback ISBN-13: 978-0615986050

Paperback ISBN-10: 0615986056

LCCN: 2014935809

Library of Congress Catalog Number: 2014935809

1. The Café 2. Apropos of the Midnight Oil

Printed in the United States of America

Notes from the Café

For Rosalie Albair Georgy

R.F. Georgy

Part I

The Café

"The author of the diary and the diary itself are, of course, imaginary. Nevertheless it is clear that such persons as the writer of these notes not only may, but positively must, exist in our society, when we consider the circumstances in the midst of which our society is formed. I have tried to expose to the view of the public more distinctly than is commonly done, one of the characters of the recent past. He is one of the representatives of a generation still living."

__Fyodor Dostoevsky

"There are more things in heaven and earth, Horatio, than are dreamt of in your philosophy. "

__Shakespeare

I

Today the virtuous doctors have confirmed my imminent death. A few weeks I'm told, perhaps days. An incurable disease of exceptional rarity, they tell me. Perhaps I will have an exceptional death; perhaps I will make a fine specimen for the specialists. Yes specialists, these virtuous experts who are eager to cut me open like a worm. But do not be alarmed, gentlemen, I was assured that my body will be useful in benefiting other worms.

But why, I must ask, do you insist upon attending an uneventful conclusion of a life so unassuming as mine? You…you wish to pay homage? But I'm afraid I don't understand. Just leave me alone. Leave me the hell alone! What? You insist upon staying. Tell me, gentlemen, what is it you want from me? Why don't you go back to your virtual cave where reality is an illusion and illusions, after all, are a click away. Isn't that what you prefer? So tell me, why have you come out of your cave? Isn't the crystal palace enough to keep you busy? Of course you know the crystal palace. You live within its infinite boundaries. Why do you look so puzzled? Just leave me alone. What's that? You heard a great deal about me? Well, I'm afraid you have me at a disadvantage. I'm not altogether certain of my own identity so I'm not sure how I can be of any service to you. What? Speak up! I'm not a young man anymore. You have been looking for me? But what could I possibly offer you, gentlemen?

You want to discuss my philosophical work? What work? I'm afraid you have me confused with someone else. I haven't written a single word of philosophical importance. Wait, you might be confusing me for that Underground fellow. I never discovered his true identity so I call him the Underground fellow. People often confuse us, but I can assure you we are quite different. Surely you've heard of the Underground Man? He lived in a chicken coop for much of his life. I grant you he is not popular today, but he caused quite a stir back in... never mind. You wouldn't understand. Do you even know who I am? The Café Dweller? Is that what people are calling me now? Well I would rather dwell in cafes than be reduced to some kind of virtual slave.

I don't think you want to talk to an old, broken down fellow who no longer fits into the scheme of things. Besides, I would do you a grave injustice if I indulge myself. It doesn't matter; you wouldn't understand what I have to say. You are too sophisticated to understand the

3

subtleties of someone who is a lifetime removed from the information age. I remember a time when information bowed down with humility before wisdom. Today, information has become pompous and arrogant. Are you with me, gentlemen? You are, after all, here to listen to what I have to say. But what you don't realize is that information paints no picture, sings no song, and writes no poem. Think about that for a minute. You look puzzled and confused. I know your confusion, gentlemen, I've seen it before. Please leave me alone. I'm a sick man, a spiteful man, and I don't think you want to deal with me.

Why did you look for me? I want to be left alone. Leave me the hell alone! Wait! You are leaving? Do you have a cigarette? If you were to offer me a cigarette, I might be willing to oblige you. What good is a café without a cigarette? You don't smoke? Of course you don't. Smoking is no longer fashionable. We smokers are an endangered species. Science no longer approves of us. We are an outcast, you understand. How the hell can anyone write without a cup of coffee and a cigarette? There are a million cafes, but what good are they? They are sterile environments where people come in to have their lattes and engage in meaningless conversations. Wait, meaningless conversation is a luxury that we don't have the time for anymore. Have you noticed what's happened to this café, gentlemen? People come here to stare at their damn tablets and laptops. Look around you and tell me what you see. Look over there, we have created a generation of virtual zombies who have no clue they are no longer human. So, do you have any cigarettes for me? You will get some? Very well, then, I will talk to you.

§§§

Ah, cigarettes at last! Do you have a light? Thank you. What is it you want to know? I suppose I'm a curiosity to you; a grotesque representation of an era that had no smart phones, computers, and instant reality. What do you mean it's him? Of course it's me, whoever me is. Did you know we live in an age where experts and specialists have become the prophets of our time, actors and sports players are mythological heroes, and mediocrity is a virtue. It was bad enough that we had to endure crystal palaces, now we have to deal with virtual palaces that exist in realities that I'm not sophisticated enough to understand. What? Speak up, I can't hear you? Oh, you want to know if I've always dwelled in cafés? I haven't always dwelled in cafés, you know. I was like you. I was ambitious, rational, logical, and successful. I don't exactly remember what I did, but I was an intellectual of some sort.

I taught philosophy? How would you know that? Funny, for some reason my memory escapes me at the moment. Tragic thing when you lose your memory, wouldn't you agree, gentlemen? What are we without our memory? We exist, I would grant you that, but what kind of existence do we lead? For some reason, I have this strange sensation, fractured and disjointed, as if reality itself is fading. Have you ever had such a sensation, gentlemen? I can assure you it is most unpleasant. I'm reminded of a physicist friend of mine who declared that reality is an illusion, albeit a persistent one. Perhaps it is an illusion, but I feel at the moment that I'm in some kind of existential black hole where all reality is sucked in, but never emerging again. What a curious sensation. I could use more coffee, gentlemen. Yes, I know you are deeply curious about what I'm about to say, but I can't have a cigarette without coffee.

Ah, a fresh cup of coffee! Nothing is quite like the aroma of a fresh cup of coffee. Why do I smoke so much? Now that's a question, gentlemen. Straight to the point, I like that. I suppose you want some sort of submissive answer, don't you? You want me to say that I know it will kill me and that I'm addicted to nicotine. You want to hear that I'm trying to stop, but too weak to succeed. Why do people give such feeble answers? Do you want to know why I smoke? I smoke in defiance to the science of our time. Yes, you heard correctly. I smoke out of spite. Science has become our new church. It is the ipso-facto intellectual authority that instructs us on all aspects of living. To hell with science and its damn method. Now, I grant you it is a pure method with stunning outcomes, but it is also a system of thought that limits my freedom. I have no use for science.

Science enlightens us? Of course you are going to say that, gentlemen. You are all children of science. You have been ensnared by its glamour and bewitching proclamations. I'm not fooled by... Never mind, Science can go to hell! Do you hear me, gentlemen. I remember an English philosopher who thought himself to be an enlightened person. His name? I don't recall, but he wrote a book, well more of a manifesto on why he is not a Christian. Do you know who I'm talking about? Very well, he suggested that the church limited our freedom and science was the only intellectual activity to liberate us from the darkness of religion. That's all very well and I agree with him that religion limits our understanding. But why does he embrace science? I mean what the hell has science done to liberate us? Science has become an all-powerful force that tells us how to live. From what toothpaste to buy to how to vote, it is science that we follow. Who the hell gave science the unilateral authority to use moral language? Explain that to me, gentlemen. You don't understand? Of course you don't understand. It is beyond your capacity to comprehend.

You see, science speaks to us in a language that is reminiscent of the church. Thou shalt not smoke. Thou shalt not eat too much fat. Thou shalt exercise. I mean, I certainly don't need science to tell me how to live. Science does this for my benefit? Oh the hell it does! Do you actually believe what you are saying, gentlemen? I need another cigarette. This is what the church did. The church would pontificate with absolute authority. We were told to trust the church; that they knew what the hell they were talking about. What do you think science does now? It pontificates from some self-righteous position of undisputed authority and we are forced to listen. You know what the doctors told me about my smoking? 'Sir, you need to stop smoking or it will kill you.' When I confronted them about their moral tone, they became agitated. It was as if how dare I question their authority. Why did I leave teaching?

§§§

I have no memory of teaching, let alone leaving. Teaching is a dying profession, did you know that, gentlemen? Who needs teachers when everything is now online. I remember a time when teachers possessed a certain level of sagacity. They had an intellectual presence and were valued for their ability to impart knowledge. Today, teachers are only there to mediate information. The digital age does not know what to do with teachers. It's funny when you consider the Luddites of the nineteenth century. They were frightened of the machines that threatened to render their factory work obsolete. What do you think the digital age is doing to teachers? Why, did you know that teachers today are controlled and manipulated by publishing companies who have an interest in transitioning all teaching activities to the virtual crystal palace?

Teachers no longer have autonomous control. They have surrendered their authority to sophisticated technocrats who are only interested in creating more technocrats to help expand and maintain the digital complex. The very idea that teaching is a noble and virtuous enterprise, whose singular aim is to transmit knowledge, is laughable. The digital age does not need teachers; no, gentlemen, the digital age needs information managers to keep our virtual palace moving along. These information managers will soon be replaced by digitized teachers who will 'facilitate' learning. Mark my words, gentlemen, teaching is dead; along with God, philosophy, cigarettes, and anything else that serves as a reminder of a past that can't be reconciled with information. What's that? You want to ask me about twice two? What a curious thing to say. Oh, I see; why is twice two sometimes a five?

Yes I know what you are thinking; the Underground Man made this same statement a hundred and fifty years ago and I'm the living proof of it. I am the five. I'm the remainder of an unbalanced equation. We are all remainders of an unbalanced equation. Twice two is a perfect summation of man, don't you agree with me? If you believe that twice two is four, then you will adapt to our glorious twenty-first century with seamless ease. What are we, gentlemen? You decide; are we a four or five? To accept we are the number four is to accept mathematical precision and the implications of what this rationally governed number has in store for us. This reminds me of a

British mathematician and philosopher who once told me he likes mathematics because it is not human and has nothing particular to do with the world or with our accidental universe. Yes, the very same philosopher who lashed out against religion.

Now, are you beginning to understand, gentlemen? Our sophisticated digital age is based on this one simple equation: Twice two is four. We have elevated the number four to a mystical realm. We have built a digital alter so that we might worship this most holy of numbers. Yes, I know that you are still confused, but allow me to elaborate. Would you agree with me that twice two is four is a perfectly harmonious equation. It is rational and not subject to the whims of human emotion. Now look at the digital age that is all around you. Tell me what you see? You don't understand? They have eyes, but cannot see! Am I religious? No, gentlemen, but do please feel free to keep up with me. Don't you understand? The digital age believes in the rational ordering of human beings. We believe that information will eventually solve every conceivable problem.

We want to ignore our emotions. We want to do away with the irrational taint that reminds us of what we once were. We want to evolve so daman fast that we have forgotten what it was like to be human. We busy ourselves with technology that we begin to actually believe in our own sophistication. Technology is changing us into something that grotesquely resembles human beings, but what we don't realize is that we are miserable creatures, cut off from a universe that does not care about our endless interrogations. We are a curiosity; I will grant you that; I would go so far as to say we are endlessly fascinating, but when we try to pretend that we are the number four, that's where I draw the line. What's that? Why do I prefer the café?

I grew tired of isolation. I needed to be around people. I lied just now, gentlemen, the truth is I don't care for people; not twenty-first century people. You see, the café is one of the few remaining places where the long, tentacle-like hands of the digital age is kept out. Look around you and tell me what you see. It is a sensory experience unlike any other. the aroma of fresh coffee, the sounds of saucers and cups, the chatter of people. It is a place where I feel alive. Can you smell the coffee? I misled you once again, gentlemen. I don't care for cafés anymore. They are a wretched place, filled with people who are pretending to be doing something important as they isolate themselves in some virtual corner. Cafés are no longer for engaging in stimulating conversation. No, gentlemen, they are designed for people to come in with their laptops and smartphones and find a corner to escape the world.

Is this what technology is designed to do? We are told these fancy gizmos offer us non-stop connection to the world. They tell us that we live in the information age. What is information, anyway? Have you thought of it? Have you given any thought to the language we freely throw about without any clue as to its meaning? We confuse information for knowledge, and knowledge that is built from information somehow passes for wisdom. People today speak in a language I no longer recognize. We no longer reflect so much as we devour information. We are consumers of information and nothing more. Modern man is not a learned creature so much as he is a slave to information. Haven't you noticed that we've become addicted to information. I should know, I am, after all, an addict myself and we addicts know the signs and symptoms of addiction.

We have an infinite supply of information and yet we cannot read. We went from the printing revolution to the visual revolution and in the process we lost our ability to think for ourselves. We require experts and specialists to think for us. We are lead to believe that we are living in a utopia; that we are enlightened. Alas! we are drowning in a sea of mediocrity. The information age is hollow and empty. It seduces us with the dizzying promise of a better tomorrow. We are like children, happy to get our toys and are willing to offer our souls in order to continue playing in the crystal palace. This is what has become of us. The Underground Man recognized what was about to happen a century and a half ago. I wonder what he would say if he were around today. I suspect he would declare the human race to be an irrelevant footnote; a cosmic accident that never should have happened.

II

Might I trouble you for another cigarette. Forgive me, gentlemen, I got carried away just now. You see I never cared for science. There is something about it that does not sit well with me. Do you know what science is? According to you, it is a rational principle, perhaps you would go so far as to say an enlightened principle. Let me tell you what science is: Science is the negation of freedom. Science is our new God; our new mathematics. You look puzzled, but don't be alarmed. You see, my good friend, the Underground Man, was wrong. Poor fellow, he thought that twice to isn't always four. Well he was wrong, gentlemen. Yes, I know what I said earlier, but I'm old and you should allow me to revel in contradiction. Science is making us all into the number four. Everything must be rational and ordered. This, after all, is the age of reason and progress.

Just look around you and you will find that our glorious twenty-first century is nothing but a sham. Yes, gentlemen, you heard me, a sham. At this point you may want to respond, but you can't. You cannot respond to what you don't understand. We don't speak the same language; you were trained for analysis, not reflection. Yes, I grant you that I was also trained for analysis, but I converted to reflection. You are experts, gentlemen, a most unfortunate development, I'm sure. You shouldn't have come here. You are not prepared for me. You see I have an advantage over you. I understand your language. I know more about you than you know about yourselves.

You believe in progress. You believe in the perfectibility of man. You believe in the rational ordering of human beings. You believe in the crystal palace. You believe in... wait, no you worship the number four. You look puzzled, I know. I speak in parables. You, gentlemen, prefer the concision of facts and figures. Let me explain what I mean by the number four. According to mathematics, twice two is always four. Isn't that a wonderfully rational statement, gentlemen? Isn't it precise and accurate? Now what has the digital age done with this statement? It has built an edifice over it. The foundation of the digital age is, after all, mathematics.

Just look around you, everything is perfectly calculated. Nothing is left to chance. Everything, every damn thing is calculated. We are no longer free, gentlemen. We are no longer free to choose. I recall a French existentialist who was fond of saying we are free to choose. The Frenchmen was wrong. Everything is predetermined for us by science almighty. Science is our new God; it is our new opiate. The Trierian didn't know that science and technology would become the opiate of the people. Science today has reduced us to numbers. Everyone is fond of the digital age, but what you don't realize, gentlemen, is that we have become digits.

I warned them, but did they listen? The specialists say I have a few days, but what do they know. I will go on living, gentlemen. Out of spite I will go on living. I will go on living to prove a point. Though I think old age is indecent, I will push on. Might I trouble you for another cigarette? What is man's nature? Surely you know man's nature. It is self-evident. Man is stupid by nature. He is stupid to the extreme and what is worse is he doesn't know his own stupidity. He thinks that because of his sophisticated toys he's become something important; that he earned his place in the universe. What science and technology have done is veil our stupidity- nothing more. You are laughing again. I can tell by your fake smiles and condescending look. Did you know that genius is found in the oddest of places?

I was wrong about cafés, gentlemen, the digital age managed to get its ugly hands in here. Do you know that I can't smoke a cigarette in here? I can drink my fancy latte, but no smoking. What good is a cup of coffee without a cigarette? How can anyone read or write in this suffocating environment? Damn these experts! They think they are so smart with their science. What's a man to do in a café without a cigarette? Twiddle his thumbs? Did you know that experts have become our new prophets? Yes, gentlemen, they have become the prophets of our time. We have an army of them telling us everything from what to eat to how to navigate the internet. Why, there are even experts that tell us how to use toilet paper. You find that funny, gentlemen? Well I can assure you it's no laughing matter. Experts tell us what to think, when to exercise, what to wear, to watch our cholesterol, to avoid caffeine, should I keep going? Wait, let me catch my breath.

Whatever problems our illustrious-twenty-first century has, it is the experts and specialists who tell us what to do. They appear on television to tell us what is good for us. I was wrong just now, gentlemen. Television is an antiquated technology. Today, we simply use our smart phone to access the world. Imagine that! the whole damn world is now at our fingertips. What? Do I have a smart phone? Yes, of course, I have a smart phone. It is a glorious device. It puts the world in the palm of my hands. You look confused. Yes, I know, I'm full of contradictions. What you don't know is that contradictions are the path to truth. Do you know what all this fancy technology has done to us? It has put us to sleep. Yes, sleep, gentlemen, and take those stupid smiles off your faces. Television has become the omniscient and omnipotent God-like technology that tells us everything from... Never mind, I've already said what I needed to.

§§§

Might I trouble you for another cigarette? I can have the whole pack? Thank you, gentlemen. Did you know I measure time with cigarettes? It's not as accurate as a watch, but it suffices. This reminds me of a philosopher friend of mine who had a ritualistic habit of walking three hours per day. Without fail, and regardless of weather, the Konigsbergian would take his walk from noon to three in the afternoon. His routine was so meticulously organized that people set their clock according to his walks. Who was he? I'm surprised you don't know who I'm talking about. He was the intellectual giant of the modern world. He was born in a Prussian town called Konigsberg, but I prefer to call him the Konigsbergian. Look at us today, we are all punctually neurotic? Remind me to come back to that point. Now where were we? Ah yes, television. Just a minute. I need a refill. Waitress! Get me a refill. What's that? There is no smoking? Listen, I've been smoking here long before you were born, so get me my damn refill! Why did she walk off like that? These young people today. Forgive me, gentlemen, you are probably anxious to hear what I have to say about television.

Let me tell you a story; a parable actually. I'm sure you're familiar with it. It was written thousands of years ago by a famous philosopher, a true philosopher, gentlemen. No, not the ugly one. It was his student. It's called the cave parable and it goes something like this. Imagine a cave where people have been chained from their neck and feet since childhood. Behind them is a fire where someone is parading figures of animal puppets. The only thing these cave dwellers can see in front of them are the shadows of these animal puppets. Are you with me so far? Good, now remember, the shadows on the wall of the cave are two-dimensional. The chief occupation of these cave dwellers is to sit there and memorize the order of the shadows. The best of them, the hero, if you will, is the one who best memorizes the order of the shadows.

That's it, gentlemen, that's the parable. Well, there is more, but this is sufficient for the point I want to make. Do you know what it means? Do you know what the philosopher was trying to say? It's all quite simple, really. You see, the cave dwellers lived in a two-dimensional reality. They lived in a state of ignorance and intellectual darkness. How am I doing so far, gentlemen? You are inspired by my wit and perspicacity, I know. I told you, genius is found in the oddest of places. Now, let's see if we can make a connection between this ancient parable and television. I'm good at making connections. You might say I'm an expert. That's what philosophers should make—connections. They should come down from their ivory towers and touch cement.

What? Ah, yes of course, the connection. Television has been hailed as a technological miracle; but it isn't really a miracle at all. Television is the modern cave. I should write a parable myself. I will call it the TVP. Everyone is fond of acronyms today. We are too lazy to utter whole words. Yes, the TVP, gentlemen, the television parable. What do you think? I can be fancy and sophisticated, too. It would go something like this: Imagine a crystal palace where people are chained by the couch. In front of them is a flat screen on the wall where two-dimensional images appear in color. These domestic dwellers can control what they see by touching a screen on their crystal pads. They sit there and memorize the order of these sophisticated images that appear before them. They pride themselves not only on memorizing the shadows, but they freely talk about the images they see. What do you think of my parable, gentlemen? I find it brilliant myself.

Do you know whoever invented television had no idea what he was about to unleash? This reminds me of the sorcerer's apprentice who, upon realizing the awesome power of his creation, said: 'Die ich rief, die Geister, Werd ich nun nicht los.' You didn't know I speak German, did you? Genius is found in the oddest of places. Now, let me... What's that? You want to know what the apprentice said? Very well, but I need another cigarette. What? Speak up! Don't whisper to each other, come out with it. Ah, I just put out a cigarette? And this troubles you? You actually care about my longevity, don't you? How so very virtuous of you! I can assure you nothing would make me happier than to depart this world with its false sophistication. What? Oh, yes the apprentice. He said, the spirits I summoned, I can't get rid of them. Do you see the parallels with television? We summoned a force which we can't contain.

Notes from the Café

What happened to us in the digital age? We used to be a useless passion, I grant you that. Today, we can't aspire to be a useless passion. We have been reduced to a microchip. The Underground Man used to say we are an organ stop. Oh what I wouldn't give to be an organ stop. The organ stop had character; it had a purpose and a function. Today we are a microchip, tomorrow we will be an avatar in some artificial world and forget that we were once a useless passion. You still don't understand the connection? Let's put some life into the Athenian's parable. You see, television has become our new alter. We gather round and worship those who populate its endless stream of mind numbing images. Television has become a ubiquitous force that has robbed us of independent thought.

III

Wait, I was wrong just now, gentlemen. The world is changing so damn fast, I can't keep up. Today, we control what we want to watch, when we want to watch, and where we want to watch. The whole damn world is now at our fingertips. Who needs television when you have a nice shiny tablet or mobile device? Don't you just love these fancy new names? Oh, what I wouldn't give to have television again! Don't misunderstand me, I hate television with a passion. Yes, I grant you it is a worthless piece of technology that conjures up shadows for our immediate consumption, but they are our shadows. I remember the day when people used to gather round to watch these dazzling images. The point, gentlemen, is that we watched together. We watched the same shadows together. Television is the greatest single technology to numb our sensibilities by controlling our thoughts. But who gives a damn! At least we were together. We were dumb as organ stops, I grant you that, but we shared and celebrated our mediocrity.

Would you believe it, gentlemen, we can't even watch the same shadows. Each of us has a tablet or

smart phone to keep us in a perpetual state of mind
numbing euphoria. Liberating? Of course you will say it is
liberating. That is not you talking, gentlemen, that is the
seductive hold that technology has over you, proudly
proclaiming and advertising its extraordinary achievements.
Tell me, what has the digital age liberated us from? We
moved from communing with the shadows to being
trapped in our own private cave. That's what the digital age
has done to us. It has given each one of us our own private
cave. This is not an ordinary cave, mind you. One might
say it is the most seductive form of hell ever devised by
man. Just look around you and tell me what you see.
Everyone is sitting about playing with their fancy gadgets.
They are sitting together, but they want nothing to do with
each other. I could use another cup of coffee.

Waitress! Where did that damn waitress go? Now
where was I? Oh yes, of course, I was responding to your
preposterous suggestion that technology is liberating us.
We have become a culture obsessed with the latest gadgets.
The whole world; the whole damn world is now in our
pockets! Hallelujah for progress! Hallelujah for science!
Liberate us indeed! Why, do you know you can watch

movies, play games, read books, purchase goods and services, find driving directions, visit virtual worlds, use virtual money, listen to music, download apps, oh and let's not forget make a phone call. And all this can be done with a gadget the size of a cigarette box. How clever we've become, gentlemen. Who needs people anymore when you have this magic box to keep you occupied for a lifetime? We have not been liberated, gentlemen, we have been imprisoned by our own arrogance. We believe we are swimming a positive course. We believe in science and the promise of a better tomorrow. We believe that our fancy gadgets will deliver us from the darkness of a chicken coop. What? You don't understand this reference? Gentlemen, you must read more.

§§§

I already told you about my underground friend who once lived in a chicken coop. He took pleasure in mocking the modern world. I grant you he was a nasty and spiteful man, but he had something to say about our glorious crystal palace. I know you are still confused about the crystal palace, but do not worry, gentlemen, it will become clear to you soon enough. You see, my friend never cared for the stubborn and immovable fact that twice two is always four. You would agree with me that this compact and yet pithy statement is the pinnacle of mathematical precision. We do not only accept that twice two is four, we celebrate its rational foundation. There is something about this extraordinarily simple equation; something so utterly simple and yet horrifyingly distant. We've become so enamored with the number four that our lives are dictated by its governing principles.

Stop looking at each other in complete and utter confusion, gentlemen. You are the ones who sought me out, remember? You will sit here and listen to what I have to say. Look at the world as it is constituted today. It is a world built on the promise that science and technology will save us. It is a world built around the number four. The only problem is that we are not a four. Did these engineers and scientists bother to stop for one minute to consider that we might be a five? Yes, you heard me, gentlemen, twice two is five. Although science may have you believe we are a four, I can assure you we are not.

We are the remainder of a fraction; a fraction that believes itself to be noble and proper. I lied just now, gentlemen, we are not worthy of being a remainder. We can't even aspire to being an irrational number. At least pi has a purpose and a function. We are the unfortunate zero that exists in the denominator of a fraction. We are undefined, a most unfortunate occurrence, I grant you. Just as the zero can be perfectly rational and harmonious, it can also be rendered undefined and meaningless. This is our existential dilemma in its bare essence, gentlemen. We delude ourselves into believing that our scientific and technological sophistication have eliminated the absurdity of our existence. Alas, our collective delusion is at an end. The absurd is never beyond reach and it is now lurking, ready to slap us back into consciousness. You are looking at each other again, gentlemen. I know this look. You are in awe of my intellect. You did not expect such perspicacity. You did not expect such brilliance to be found in a broken down café. Genius is found in the oddest of places.

You don't believe our lives are absurd? Well, of course, you don't. You believe our existence is perfectly managed and ordered. You believe in the perfectibility of man; in his infinite wisdom to rationally direct his own future. But what you don't understand, gentlemen, is the absurd is a basic principle of human existence. If only we listened to my Algerian friend. Well, he was not really

Algerian; more French than Algerian. You are not familiar with him? Of course you're not. Why would you be? He wrote a brilliant book on the absurd, the Myth of something or other, I don't remember the rest of the title, but I can assure you he was brilliant. Poor fellow died in a car accident, which in itself is an absurdity of the highest order.

What do I mean? I'll tell you what I mean. He never cared for automobiles. He would never drive one or be driven in one. Would you believe it, on that one singular occasion when someone offered to drive him, the car hits a tree, killing them both. A fitting end for someone who made it his business to describe the absurd dies an absurd death. Do you know what he once told me before his early demise? He told me the absurd is the fundamental concept and the first truth. It is the absurd that links us to the world. Ah, one of you has a question. I was wondering If you were actually listening to me. Very well, what is your question? What is the role of the absurd in the modern world? Gentlemen, I'm impressed. I didn't think you were listening.

Consider this; our existence is inherently absurd. We are the children of chance and probability; we are the probabilistic outcome of randomized motion. Now, you may consider this to be the absurd, but you would be wrong. The absurd dwells within our consciousness. The absurd dwells in the intersection of our awareness of two fundamental and irreconcilable facts. Fact number one is that we simply exist without purpose or a governing blueprint as to why. The second stubborn fact of our miserable existence is the impenetrable door of silence. We are condemned to knock on this door only to be slapped silly. Do you know who is slapping us silly? It is the absurd. The absurd is the horrifying feeling that we are alone in a cold and uncaring universe. We cannot penetrate our existential mystery and yet we are condemned to endeavor to find meaning. The absurd is perfectly comfortable in the interstitial space of our enigmatic existence.

But let me ask you a question, gentlemen. Suppose the answers to all of our existential interrogation are offered to us on a silver platter, how would we respond? I mean, how would we react to such a revelation? Do you suppose man would be perfectly content with the answers to all of life's mystery? I'll let you in on a little secret, gentlemen. Man will never be satisfied with an answer. We fool ourselves into believing that we are interrogative creatures. We ask teleological questions as if we truly want to hear the answer. We are condemned to only ask. We don't want to know the answers. We are restless beings, gentlemen, or, if you like, we are contingent. We are not self-explanatory. Consciousness is a stubborn thing, you understand. What is my point? My point? How so very droll of you, gentlemen.

You are men of facts and figures. You want to quantify everything. You are digital zombies with an endless appetite for information. How could you possibly understand philosophy? What you fail to understand is that I don't have a point. I only offer observations on the human condition. Everything today is framed as a problem and every problem must have a solution. We live in a problem-solution age. We believe in our ability to solve all of our problems. But consider this, gentlemen, human existence is not reducible to a problem with a ready-made solution. Existence is messy and insoluble. There, I used a scientific term though I despise science.

IV

Y ou were told I despise science? Gentlemen, you seem to have me at a disadvantage. Well I do despise science, but not for any reasons you would understand. I need another cigarette. Why do you look uncomfortable whenever I light a cigarette? The sign? What sign? Oh that one. I don't give a damn about the no smoking sign. People are leaving? Let them leave. To hell with science with its self-righteous proclamations! Who the hell gave science the authority to restrict my freedom? Science is a method? How naïve you are, gentlemen, to actually believe that science is a method. I can assure you it is much more than a method. Science has become the dominant intellectual force of our time. How do you like that bit of sophistication, gentlemen? I told you, genius is found in the oddest of places.

I know what you are going to ask so I will oblige an explanation. From the cradle to the grave, our lives are dictated by science. Science determines how we should live. Thou shalt not smoke! Thou shalt exercise! Thou shalt seek psychological therapy! Forgive me for raising my voice, gentlemen, but it is frustrating to think of science as an all-powerful force. Here is a bold statement for you: Science has become the functional replacement for God. We have gone from one omnipotent force to another. We are too sophisticated to believe in fairytales.

This reminds me of my German friend who declared God dead. He was often misunderstood and misquoted. He believed that faith in God was incompatible in the age of progress. The only problem, of course, is that he declared the death of God too early. The metaphor should have been: God is ill. That would have been more appropriate, don't you agree? Riddles? I can assure you that I'm speaking the truth. Faith in God has been declining for some time now. It is we the sophisticated ones of the twenty-first century that have finally killed God. Do you understand what I'm telling you, gentlemen? God is no more. The coffin is sealed and lowered to the ground.

God is no longer an animating force in our hearts. He is obsolete. We the moderns, with all of our sophistication, have no need for him. Today, in our brave new world of the internet, social media, and shiny gadgets, God has become an anachronism. Are you with me so far? We no longer need God to answer the worn-out interrogatives of our existence. Who needs God to explain our cosmological mystery when we have quantum mechanics and the unifying theory? Who needs to pray to God when we have science almighty to solve our problems? Today we have more faith in the surgeon's hand than we in do in God.

You know what I find ironic, gentlemen? It was not philosophy that killed God. It's funny really when you contemplate this divine irony. Many philosophers have had a certain level of contempt for God. God not only defied syllogistic logic, he seemed to also defy every epistemic attempt to find a place for him in a rationally governed world. Philosophers could not accommodate him. I once knew a French mathematician who published a treatise on celestial mechanics. When he was asked by the emperor as to why he made no mention of God in his calculations, his reply was that he simply had no need for that hypothesis. No need indeed. What arrogance, gentlemen.

The God of philosophy became an unnecessary hypothesis. God was a problematic figure and a burden. If Philosophers couldn't accommodate him, then it was easier to get rid of him altogether. In order to resolve his insoluble nature, God was axiomatically removed from the world of serious discourse. As philosophers were busy reducing God to an irrelevant construction, the rest of us continued to cling to the nostalgic memory of a divine force who gave meaning to our miserable lives. Philosophy, with all of its intellectual sophistication, was incapable of posing any serious threat to the God of the masses. No gentlemen, philosophy merely paved the way for a much more powerful force. As soon as science began to flex its muscle and dazzle us with its technological wizardry, God was in trouble.

§§§

Our illustrious twenty-first century has finally buried God six feet under without any hope of resurrection. Our hands are stained; stained with the blood of our father, may he rest in peace. Mourn with me, gentlemen, we need to mourn together. I miss God already. I grant you he was an epistemically complicated thing for us to grasp, but he was necessary and useful. Who do these philosophers with their fancy logic think they are? Do you know I once had a German friend who... what? Oh, not the one who declared God dead. No, this friend, well he was not a true friend, you might say we studied philosophy together, was actually born in one of the oldest cities in Germany. Which one? Let's see if you could deduce the city, gentlemen, after all, I can't make you passive listeners. I called him the Trierian.

He was an ill-tempered fellow who always tried to borrow money from me. What does this have to do with God? Patience, gentlemen, I'm getting to it. Many years ago, this was before your time, we met in a café in Paris. Those were the days when a café meant something. Those were the days when intellectuals roamed freely without being persecuted for having a conversation over coffee and cigarettes. In any event, we discussed God for several hours. He was convinced that God was a construction designed to keep the masses in a perpetual state of subaltern existence. He likened religion to a drug that kept people in a state of euphoric submission. I find it quite extraordinary that intellectuals dismiss God simply as a... What? How did the conversation go with the Trierian? Oh, I disagreed with him, he pounded his fist on the table as he usually did, and called me an idiot. That was the last time I saw him.

You are surprised to hear I knew him. I know you are. You know, gentlemen, he was not the only one to argue that God is a construction. There was another fellow; I believe he was a Viennese physician, who argued that

God is an infantile projection needed to shield us from the mystery of a world that was at once impenetrable and frightening. This illusion, as he called it, would become unnecessary as man uses science to understand his world. Here is the problem I'm having with the construction argument. Let's assume for a moment that God is indeed a construction of the imagination. Does this mean that God has no value to us? What does it mean to say something is constructed? Does it mean the object of our construction is thoroughly debunked and is no longer necessary?

Let me ask you a question, gentlemen. Is mathematics a construction? Do you believe that a minimum of two points form a line? Of course you do, but why do you believe it? There is no proof offered and yet we believe it. If we accept that mathematics is a construction, then should it not be debunked and ignored as a topic of serious contemplation? That would be silly, of course, and mathematicians would be up in arms. The fact that something is constructed does not, in and of itself, lessen its value. What does it matter anymore, the death of God is a fait accompli. What's that, Proof?

What an extraordinary question, gentlemen? You actually want proof for the existence of an idea that is dead

and buried? Spoken like true skeptics. Before I respond to
your clever question, let me ask you one of my own.
Suppose I offer you a proof that satisfies you, what then?
What will you do with that knowledge? Will you
immediately get on your knees and pray for forgiveness?
Does the heart open its infinite embrace once the intellect
is satisfied? This is where you are wrong, gentlemen.
People do not believe in the divine as an outcome of
carefully examining the evidence. People believe in God as
an existential necessity.

I'm willing to bet, although I detest gambling with
a passion, that you, gentlemen, are agnostics. Am I correct
in making this assumption? I thought as much. Did I tell
you about the time I was invited to attend one of the
meetings of the Metaphysical Society in London?
Gentlemen, stop scratching your heads and listen to me.
You came in search of my wisdom and so you shall have it.
Why do you look stunned? What is it? Oh, you heard of
the metaphysical society? How could I…? How could I
have attended? I'm much older than you can possibly
imagine. During this meeting, which was attended by some
of the leading intellectuals of the day, a discussion arose
concerning the proof of God's existence. Would you
believe it, the atheists and theists were locked in a bitter

debate over God. One gentleman, who was referred to as the bulldog, stood up and introduced an entirely new term to describe our inability to intellectually penetrate the divine mystery.

Why was he called a bulldog? He was a clever debater with a tongue that lashed at your intellect until you submitted to his will. I remember watching him debate some English bishop over evolution. The poor bishop was out of his element. Do you know what I later discovered, gentlemen? The debate marked the first time the church publicly engaged science and, typical of the church, it embarrassed itself beyond measure. What did you say? Oh, agnosticism? I'm getting to it, gentlemen; my, but you are an impatient lot. In any event, the bulldog stood up and introduced an entirely new method of engaging metaphysical concepts. He called his method agnosticism. Little did this fellow know that God was on his way out. It's funny really when you consider that God was handed his coat and hat and shown the door just as the clever intellectuals were busy fighting for his identification. The agnostic view that developed out of that meeting was a rather benign indifference towards God.

The agnostics claim that if you are to affirm the existence of God as objective truth, then the burden is to offer evidence which will justify your certainty. You are nodding your heads in agreement, gentlemen. I don't blame you in the least. In fact, I nodded my head in agreement when I first heard the bulldog speak. It seems rather fair, doesn't it? Another way of expressing the agnostic view is that one can neither affirm nor deny the existence of God. What? Speak up, I'm not a young man anymore. I'm describing negative atheism? Of course I am, but the agnostic wants nothing to do with this vile label. The agnostic wants to maintain humility while simultaneously avoiding God. Agnosticism offers a way out, doesn't it? An agnostic doesn't want to get his hand dirty. He wants to sit back and wait for the evidence. I respect the atheist. The atheist will tell you in your face that you are a moron for believing in God.

The agnostic will demand proof before he submits to the divine order of things. What's wrong with that, you say? I will tell you what is wrong with it. How the hell do you know what the proof should look like in order to acknowledge it as the proof you require? Do you see the extraordinary arrogance in demanding proof? We have assumed all along that those who require proof have no responsibility other than to sit back, relax and wait for something extraordinary to slap them into believing. We have been lead to believe the onus of proof is on those who affirm unsubstantiated claims. What you don't realize, gentlemen, is that those who demand proof have a greater burden placed upon them. So, I ask you again, how will you know what the proof for God should look like when it is offered to you? Think about this question for a minute while I get more coffee. Where is the damn waitress? There she is. Get me a refill. Waitress! Why did she walk off like that? To hell with her, I'm getting my own coffee. I'll be back, gentlemen.

V

The service in this café is unbelievable. Do you know I've been coming here for years? I need another cigarette. Now, where were we, gentlemen? Oh yes, the concept of proof. Well, what do you think of my question? It's clever if I do say so myself. Remember, genius is found in the oddest of place. You don't understand the question? I didn't expect you to. You are eager for an explanation. I can see it in your eyes. How rational it is for someone to demand proof. After all, extraordinary claims require extraordinary evidence. Let me ask you a question. Do you know what the request means? What do we mean when we demand proof? Agnosticism, on the face of it, seems straight forward enough, but when you probe deeper you find it is an epistemological nightmare. Now I want you to listen carefully to me, gentlemen. I'm going to say this in fancy philosophical language and then simplify it for your average mind. After all, I don't want you to think you are sitting with some lunatic in a café.

Don't take offense, gentlemen. There is nothing wrong with being average anymore. We have become a culture that celebrates mediocrity. If you want to know the

one singular aim of technology, then it is this: The purpose
of technology is to keep all of us in a perpetual state of
mediocrity. We are neither illiterate peasants nor
intellectuals. I got it, gentlemen. I just had an epiphany! We
are all half-baked digits who neither want nor care about
anything other than the pursuit of more technology. We
are too sophisticated for God and we certainly don't know
what to do with philosophers who sit in a café with a cup
of coffee in one hand and a cigarette in the other. We have
cleansed ourselves from the mythological ignorance of the
past. We demand... No, we need the illusion of
sophistication in order to feel that we are worthy of the
information age. But I digress again, gentlemen.

When we demand proof, are we fully aware of
what it is we are insisting upon? What is the epistemic
framework under which a proof is rendered valid or
invalid? That's the fancy part, just in case you missed it.
Here is the simple version: How do you want the proof to
like in order to be satisfied that God does indeed exist?
What will satisfy you, gentlemen? If I parade a thousand
proofs for your intellectual consideration, how will you
know which proof is the one that you've been looking for?
It is one thing to demand proof, but a different matter
altogether to recognize it. Here is an analogy, gentlemen, so

that you may fully ponder the consequences of being an agnostic.

Let's suppose that mathematicians are given a theorem to prove. Actually, we don't have to suppose. I have an interesting story for you. Many years ago when I was a young man I met this French lawyer who prided himself on being an amateur mathematician. Actually, he was not an amateur at all. He took pleasure in identifying himself as an amateur, which brought him recognition. In some respect his work on calculus predates that English fellow who became famous for his principia as well as the German mathematician who believed he developed calculus first. In any event, the French amateur would often correspond with his learned friends by offering theorems without proof. On one occasion, he scribbled a theorem inside the margins of a book. Ah, you know who I'm talking about? I'm impressed, gentlemen. Yes, yes, it became known as his last theorem.

Now, you are aware that some Princeton professor solved the theorem, yes? You have seen a documentary on television? Did I not tell you, gentlemen, that television is the greatest invention ever devised by man. Television indeed! Now where was I? What? Who is behind me? Oh, I see. Yes, what is it? I'm in the middle of a critical point. You are the manager? What can I do for you? My smoking? Listen, I'm sick and tired of people telling me where I can smoke. Do you know I can't even smoke outside? Just a few years ago I was able to sit outside and enjoy a cigarette, but that was taken away from me. Now you have a smoke-free environment. How so very sterile of you. Listen, I'm going to smoke my cigarette, so stop disturbing me while I'm visiting these fine gentlemen. Call the police? Do whatever the hell you want, now get the hell out of my face.

Gentlemen, I'm going to light up a cigarette and if you want to leave, then I suggest you do so. You will stay? How so very brave of you. I seem to have lost my train of thought. Mathematical proofs? Oh yes, of course. When the Princeton professor proved the Frenchman's last theorem, his proof was subjected to scrutiny by other esteemed mathematicians from around the world. Patience, gentlemen, I'm getting to it. What do you think these mathematicians used to verify the proof? They used the governing rules of mathematics to check for any errors. Don't you see, there was a framework; a kind of epistemic test to determine the veracity of the proof. Now, what kind of framework should we use to assess metaphysical evidence?

Consider, if you will, the different knowledge domains we have at our disposal. You have mathematical knowledge, scientific knowledge, literary knowledge, historical knowledge, theological knowledge, and so on. Now, which knowledge domain do you wish to use to examine the various proofs for the existence of God? You can't use all of them, of course, as one area of knowledge will contradict another. The scientific method? That's what the agnostics have always assumed when they demanded proof, but I have a simple question, gentlemen. Why science? Why have we elevated science to such a degree that it has become the unquestioned authority in all intellectual matters? I grant you science has something to say about the physical world, but why does it unilaterally assume it has authority over all other knowledge domains? Doesn't it seem to you that all other sources of knowledge must bow down to the self-evident superiority of science?

I must also remind you that science offers us probabilistic knowledge. This once fledgling method, whose noble mission was to liberate the human mind from the bondage of revealed knowledge, has now become a ubiquitous force that instructs us on all aspects of living. If science can't grant God permission to exist, then God doesn't exist. It's that simple, gentlemen. What does it matter anyway? Whether you believe in an omniscient and omnipotent ontological being or you accept the construction argument, both are dead. We no longer believe in such nonsense. So now I ask you, gentlemen, what do we need God for? Faith? Faith is a private matter? How diplomatic of you. I'm actually glad you responded in this way. I'm proud of myself, gentlemen. Are you aware that you fell into my trap? Faith is indeed a private affair. That's what ultimately killed God, the privatization of faith.

§§§

Once faith left the public square, it would only be a matter of time before God was on his way out. It is no longer fashionable to speak of God in public. In fact, I dare say it has become an altogether indecent thing to mention God. What? You have a question for me? Well go on! I'm not getting any younger. Do I believe in God? I do believe in God, and do you know why? Spite, that's right, spite. Out of spite for science I will cling to an illusion. I may not want to have anything to do with God, but I will believe in him. If I have to choose between the comfort of a myth and the cold, probabilistic wasteland of science, I choose the myth. Not what you expected? Well, what did you expect? You heard I'm an atheist? I'm sorry to disappoint you; gentlemen, but I can assure you that I am not.

How could I believe in God if...? If what, gentlemen? I see, how could I believe in God if he is dead and buried, is that what you are asking me? I am a man of contradiction. I'm entitled to contradict myself; after all I'm old and don't have the time or patience for clarity. I consider myself an intellectual who has something to say. A rare thing we intellectuals have become. We too are a dying breed. Today we live in the age of experts and specialists. Experts and specialists have become the prophets of our time. But I am not fooled, gentlemen, for I see through them. They are false prophets, you understand. Everyone today is an expert. The information age has no room for intellectuals. Information needs experts to organize, catalogue, manipulate, and control its mind numbing bits of data. We intellectuals are ponderous and slow. We are obsolete in a world that celebrates the efficient and rapid fire speed of information.

Notes from the Café

Listen to this story, gentlemen, and you will be amazed at how fast intellectuals fell from grace. In the not too distant past, I found myself attending a lecture on religious experience at the University of Edinburgh in Scotland. What's that? Yes, I do get around, gentlemen. You should come back and visit me and I will tell you all about my travels. In any event, the lecturer was a Harvard professor who... what is it now? You heard of this professor? Yes, that's him. His brother was a novelist of considerable reputation. What I found interesting about the lecture was the audience. The vast majority of them were physicians. Now, you may not find this to be of any particular interest, but it signaled the beginning of the end for us intellectuals. These physicians were attending a lecture by someone defending religious experience.

What I'm trying to say, gentlemen, is that these physicians and scientists were also the intellectuals of the day. They engaged in ideas that went beyond their vocation. They were learned men; men of science, I grant you, but they were intellectuals. Now, answer this simple question: Can you imagine a similar lecture today that concerns itself with philosophy, literature, religion, and so on, where the audience is primarily composed of scientists? It would be preposterous to think of such a thing in the digital age. Do you know what the Bostonian did during his lecture? He admonished the audience for embracing the materiality of this world and ignoring the possibility of transcendent experience. He warned them not to use science to hide behind agnosticism. Now, what do we do today? We celebrate science while giving lip service to all that is transcendent. We are living in the age of false prophets and there isn't a damn thing you can do about it. Hallelujah! Experts are now the new priestly class and deserve our respect.

VI

My head! My head! What is this sensation? Where am I? Who are you people? No, I'm not alright. Suddenly I have this sense that I don't belong here. Why are you here again? I feel disoriented and confused. Why are you here? We've been having a philosophical conversation? I have no memory of that. Leave me alone. This place somehow does not feel real to me. It has the contours of reality, but something is missing. I feel a disturbing sense of cerebral detachment from the physicality of life. What an odd sensation. Are you gentlemen still here? Suddenly I feel sleepy. What's that? I can't sleep? Why not? I'm an old man and deserve some sleep. You might say I've earned the right to sleep. You came a long way to see me? Very well, gentlemen, what do you want to see me about? We were talking about experts? I don't remember talking to you about anything. You want to know why I don't care for experts? How did you know this about me? I just told you? What kind of nonsense is this? I do dislike experts, gentlemen, I dislike them with a passion.

Did you know that experts and specialists have become... Why do I feel that I'm being redundant? No matter, everyone is a damn expert today. Why, do you know when they diagnosed my condition, there were a team of doctors busy trying to figure out what ails me. Whenever I had a question, I was referred to the appropriate specialists. When they couldn't find an answer, I was told that medicine is on the verge of a breakthrough. How so very comforting to hear that, gentlemen. For some reason I don't remember what they diagnosed me with, but I don't really care. I'm actually glad to be leaving this prison called the digital age. I'm an anachronistic fool who overstayed his welcome. The twenty-first century does not want nor can tolerate Neo-Luddites who are antiquated and obsolete. I am a reminder of a past that people want to forget. I am a reader of books. I am a coffee drinking, chain smoking writer who overstayed his welcome. Why did I say I'm a writer? I'm not sure, but for some reason I believe that I was once a writer.

In any event, can you imagine all these specialists desperately trying to keep one more miserable worm alive just a little longer. We are obsessed with the physicality of our existence. We go to great extremes to cure disease, increase longevity, improve our appearance, and all to make us forget that our lives are absurd. Yes, I'm back to the absurd if you don't mind. You see, gentlemen, the absurd has never left us. It is always there; always lurking beneath the surface, ready to strike at any time. We believe that if we drown our existence in technology that we will somehow change our nature. That's the premise of the twenty-first century, to use technology to help us forget our true nature. If religion was once used to keep people in a state of darkness, then technology today is an equivalent mind-numbing drug. Rather than use religion to escape the unbearable heaviness of our existence, we use our crystal tablets and smart phones to escape the true meaning of who we are.

I remind you of the Czech writer? So you are listening, gentlemen, I'm impressed. Actually, the writer you are referring to prefers to be known as a French writer. He is one of the last remaining intellectuals alive today. I had coffee with him years ago in Paris. We discussed the concept of Being. He believes our existence is light as a feather. He rejected the German philosopher's idea of eternal recurrence. Yes, gentlemen, the same German philosopher who declared God dead. The German argued that if our lives are in a state of eternal recurrence, then our existence is unbearably heavy. His solution was to embrace our fate. The Czech, of course, rejected this premise and embraced a linear existence where we only have one shot at this life. This one singular attempt at life that could just as easily have not happened at all is the reason for our lightness. You are suddenly quiet, gentlemen. I seem to have your rapt attention. Did I agree with him?

Of course I didn't agree with him. Both the German and the Czech were wrong. There is no reason to believe in eternal recurrence, no reason at all. I suppose if you want to believe in an illusion that gives your life a sense of continuity and enduring meaning, then you should hold on to this myth of circular life. I accept that life, absurd as it is, is a singular experience. In this respect I agree with the Czech, but what I fail to understand is why would that make our lives ethereal? It is the density of our lives that gives rise to the absurd. Now I seem to have confounded you, gentlemen. I will explain myself before I lose you altogether. Within the fleeting and compact nature of our lives is a restlessness that constantly weighs on us. This restless nature, which is built into our consciousness, creates a certain density that builds over time. It is at the moment we realize that our existence defies any and all explanations that the absurd slaps us across the face to remind us that we are freaks of the universe.

Notes from the Café

You don't understand what this has to do with the Czech writer? Allow me to be more direct. The density of our existence is the result of the endless choices and interrogations that have a way of weighing on us. With each passing day our existence becomes unbearably heavy. Do you know what makes it unbearable? It is the absurd laughing at our inability to find meaning. In the end, our existence, dense as it is, fades into oblivion. This is our existential legacy: We come unto existence, make some noise and, without so much as having a clue as to what it was all for, we return to the silence that was. It is the noise we make that burdens us with a heaviness that screams out for answers. Alas, there are no answers. What's that? Religion offers us answers to these insoluble questions?

§§§

You should say that religion offered us answers. Religion has become a graveyard for the comfortable mythologies that we once embraced to shield us from the truth of our existence. Do you remember the Viennese physician I mentioned to you a few minutes ago? I hate to admit it, gentlemen, but he was right all along. He told us that as civilization advances sufficiently to answer the mystery of our existence, religion would be exposed as an illusion borne of our childlike fear of the unknown. The only problem is the good doctor encouraged this outcome. So here we are, gentlemen, living in the very future he predicted. We are now living our lives in naked isolation, ready and prepared to confront the mystery of our existence rationally and scientifically. Who needs childish mythologies when we have science to guide us? What we don't yet understand, gentlemen, is that science has become our new mythology. Science is a construction of reality, designed to control and manipulate the world by promising us a utopia here on earth.

Science has delivered on its promise? Of course it has. Who in their right mind would deny that science improved our lives? But the comforts of science and the spectacular gadgets we use come at a price. It's a price I'm not willing to pay. Do you hear me, gentlemen? Do you remember the English philosopher I mentioned earlier, the one who explained to us why he is not a Christian? He was a true intellectual, but he could not see the power and arrogance of science. He believed that science would be the liberator of human ignorance. He didn't appreciate that religion offered us moral instruction without offering us an explanation. Now, let me ask you a question: What the hell is science doing today? We are bombarded with the moral language of science. It is one thing for science to tell us the consequences of our actions, but when it tells us how to live, then that is power. What? Science tells us these things for our benefits?

I perfectly agree with you, but can't we apply this same response to religion. Can't we say that religion offered us moral instruction for our benefit? Science has evidence to back up its claims? Perfect, gentlemen, you are becoming true debaters. Religion can make the same claim. What did religious scholars and theologians tell us? Trust us, we have thousands of years of theological wisdom and we know what we are talking about when we give moral instructions. Well, what do you think science is doing today? The experts say the exact same thing. Trust us, we have numerous studies to support what we are telling you. We can examine the studies ourselves? No, gentlemen, we cannot. We don't have the requisite knowledge for that sort of thing. Science wants us to trust its infinite wisdom. Don't you see, gentlemen, don't you understand? Science is a construction and it has become all powerful.

Do you remember the Algerian I talked about? Well he had a friend who popularized existentialism. He became famous for his work, Being and… something or other, I don't quite remember. He and the Algerian became close friends until they parted ways. It was a shame really. Both men were intellectuals of the highest order. Did you know that when the Algerian was killed in the car accident, it was the Frenchman who gave the eulogy? This French existentialist was fond of saying that our lives have no meaning save for the sum total of choices and actions we accumulate over a lifetime. When people would ask him how they should live their lives, his only response was to choose. He told people to simply choose. This sounds well intentioned, but it's an empty counsel. Ask yourselves, gentlemen, if any of us today truly choose anything.

We have the illusion of choice, that's all that we can hope for. Science makes all of our choices for us. In fact, science tells us that choice is an illusion. Haven't you heard that conscious decisions are made pre-cognitively. You look dumb founded, but I will explain. What we once believed to be volition is nothing but neuro-chemical activity performed at a subconscious level. This is what we are told by the experts. These experts and social engineers, in their infinite wisdom, have succeeded in controlling and manipulating what we believe. We are being re-engineered as we speak. Just look at how the internet has changed us. How? How what? Oh, the internet? Let me tell you this, gentlemen, the internet is the single greatest technological revolution since the printing press.

The difference, of course, is the printing press helped usher in the enlightenment. What the hell has the internet done? It has enormous power, I grant you, but what has it done to us? All it did is drown us in an ocean of information. We are all drowning in information, but we are not aware of it. This is the seductive hold that technology has over us. It gives us the illusion of progress. Let's look at what we can do online: we can search information, read the newspaper, watch movies, purchase anything we want, read reviews, pay bills, monitor our money, publish books, and the list goes on and on. You can do all this without being tied down to a computer. A simple laptop, tablet, or smart phone can connect you to the world. These are God-like powers, mind you, but we have become so accustomed to them that we forget the extraordinary power we have at our fingertips. What's that? Everything I described is for our benefit?

VII

This is where you are wrong, gentlemen. We are seduced by the bright lights of technology, but if you delve deeper, you will find that underneath the crystal palace we've created lies a forbidden secret. Despite the explosion of information that you see all around you, we have not intellectually advanced one inch. What am I trying to say? I'm trying to tell you that reflection is dead as a result of information. I'm trying to tell you that you can keep your crystal palace. I'm perfectly content living in a chicken coop. What's that? What is it about technology that bothers me? Everything! Everything about technology bothers me. I never cared for fancy gadgets that pretend to be something more. Technology has changed us into something grotesquely distorted. Do you know that I no longer recognize my fellow man as human?

Oh, it starts innocently enough. You don't notice it at first. When cell phones came out, they were bulky things that only the rich could afford. As the size grew smaller, the cost came down and, in a blink of an eye, everyone had a cell phone. The same was true of computers. I remember a time when they were too bulky to belong anywhere but libraries, the military, and industry. In no time at all, every damn household had a personal computer. But that was not enough, you see, the inexorable movement of technology would keep going. Today, the personal computer converged with the cell phone to create the smart phone. In fact, the PC, as you, gentlemen, prefer to call it, is becoming obsolete. We prefer our mobile devices, but that, too, will soon change. Perhaps in the future we will become part man, part machine. You are laughing now, but wait and see. They will place the computer directly into our brains. Do you know what bother me?

It is not technology per se. It is how we relate to it. We don't pause and reflect on what we are doing. We simply embrace every new innovation that is thrown at us. Those who question it are looked upon as Luddite radicals who are in the way of inevitable progress. Human progress is now defined only in terms of scientific and technological innovation. We don't care how technology operates as long as it makes our lives easier. This was the same for religion. We didn't care if the theology stood up to rigorous scrutiny. As long as religion gave us a sense of hope and a self-contained meaning, we embraced it. We pride ourselves on the notion that we have moved beyond the darkness of the cave, but what we don't realize is that we have created our own artificial cave. Our lives are hectic and we move at such an alarming speed that we have no time to ponder anything. Time itself has been dissected to such a degree that everything is planned and accounted for.

We have become an extension of the technology we create. Have you noticed how people text? They are oblivious to the world. Do you know that texting is making us lose the richness of language? Who the hell cares about language anymore? We have reduced language to its skeletal makeup, which is what technology requires. Do you know what the irony is, gentlemen? You would think with the information explosion currently underway that we would all be intellectual giants. Alas, we are dumber than a chicken running around with its head chopped off. We like to fool ourselves that we are more advanced than previous generations, but I can assure you, gentlemen, that we are not. We cover up our massive shortcomings by pretending that we have access to an infinite supply of information that previous generations could only dream of. All we have to do is download any book that we want to read. How so very efficient we've become. The only problem is that with all this damn efficiency, we forgot how to read. I don't care for computers, gentlemen, and I will not be seduced by the promise of halcyon days. What's that? Computers are simply a tool?

§§§

That's a laugh, gentlemen. Wait, you actually believe what you are saying. Computers are the reason we have all become the number four. We have bought into the computer revolution lock, stock and barrel. There was a time when religion dazzled us with stories of miracles, but all the miracles in recorded history pale in comparison to what computers can do. You see, the power of computers lies in their ability to dazzle us. That's what we human beings respond to. We like to be entertained by a dog and pony show and computers have succeeded in mesmerizing us. Would you agree with me that a hammer is a tool? I thought you would. Now, humor an old man for a minute. Would you say that a hammer is in the same category as a computer? Of course you wouldn't, and yet you insist that machines which operate at the speed of light are simply tools. That's not what you meant? What did you mean, then? Ah, computers are designed to make our lives easier; yes, of course, I know what you mean. What do you think I've been trying to tell you?

Computers have made our lives just a bit too easy, wouldn't you say? Think of it, gentlemen, every category of human activity has moved to the virtual world. We don't experience the world the way we did in my day. We don't think the same way, talk the same way, read the same way, and we certainly don't reflect anymore. I grant you, the internet connects us in a way that we couldn't even dream of fifty years ago. We call this progress, but I want nothing to do with it. Do you know what the digital age does to people who do not conform to its rational principles? This God forsaken age buries you alive. Laugh if you will, gentlemen, but I speak the truth. I remember this fellow who taught literature years ago. He was a brilliant lecturer and well respected by students and faculty alike. One year, the university where he was teaching decided to transition all teaching related activity to the online world. This meant the old cranky professor had to have a web page, make his lectures available online, as well as submit his grades online. For thirty years he wrote his grades into a nicely bound notebook. He decided to put his foot down and continued to teach the same way he always did. Do you know what the university did?

They let him go. Do you know how he was let go? They sent him an email informing him that his services were no longer required. Of course, he never read his emails and they had to interrupt his lecture to politely ask him to leave. This is the dark side of progress that no one wants to talk about. I suppose if he was teaching today, he would get a text message on his smart phone. Technology today is the most alienating force in history. It's like a drug; once you get a taste of it you want more. The only problem is that when you get more, you feel a sense of unease and disquiet. The neurotic pace at which technology is changing keeps all of us in a state of perpetual euphoria, waiting for the next big thing. The toys we buy today will become obsolete in a few months. If you fail to keep up, then you will become obsolete as well. Don't you understand, gentlemen? Don't you see? We created a dystopian society that is packaged and presented to us as the inevitable outcome of progress. We interact with machines more than we do with humans. Why do you look so puzzled? Isn't this the world you live in? Let me describe to you a typical day in the crystal palace.

VIII

You wake up with an alarm clock, of course, push a button to turn on the television, go to your laptop to check emails, weather report, and read the news of the day. As you are driving to work, you feel compelled to respond to a couple of trivial text messages. While at work, you are interacting with a computer screen for much of the day. You leave work to stop by the market and use the self-checkout to pay for your food. Once you are home you decide to pay a few bills online and find there is a problem with the amount. You call customer service, but there is no one there to talk to you. Instead there is a programmed voice that helps you navigate a menu of options. Exasperated, you hang up and you blame the problem on poor customer service. Now let's examine this typical day. The person I just described can be anyone of us. Ask yourself how much human interaction did this person have. Are you beginning to understand what I mean by the crystal palace? The Underground Man may have rejected the crystal palace of the nineteenth century, but I wonder what he would say about digital palace of today.

Notes from the Café

Oh what I wouldn't give for the crystal palace of old. Today we devised an ingenious method of keeping everyone busy in in their own private cave. Do you know what this method is? Mobility? I must apologize to you, gentlemen, you are far brighter than I assumed. The wizards behind this utopia found an ingenious way to allow us to take our virtual cave with us. Wherever we go the internet is at our fingertips. Did you know that you can now have the internet planted into your cranium? Yes, I know you laughed at this suggestion before, but Haven't you heard of these new glasses that allow you to roam the internet? I told you, we are becoming internet zombies with a voracious appetite for information. We believe that information is an enlightening agent, but I can assure you it is not. We consume information, but we can't read. We forgot how to sit down and engage the dense layers of a text. We are so busy devouring information that we forgot how to dance with ideas. We confuse linguistic bits of data for knowledge and ideas. I can assure you, gentlemen, they are not the same. Ideas require effort and the kind of sensibility that engages the subtle layers of meaning. What the hell does information require? Information is what we make of it? Is that all you can muster as anything resembling a response?

Information is not what we make of it, gentlemen. Information defines us. Information shapes us. Information envelopes us and reduces us to an irrelevant afterthought. To hell with information and its seductive hold on our imagination. I'm better off chasing chickens. The chicken coop, after all, had character. What the hell happened to the chicken coop? I'm asking you, gentlemen! One day, the world was as it should be and the next it turned upside down. There was no warning. There was no damn warning! I'm free to yell if I want, so leave me the hell alone! To hell with you and this God forsaken age we live in! I will not calm down! Who the hell are you? I need another cigarette. Something very strange is going on around here. Everything looks real, but something is different. Do you ever have a feeling that you are losing your grip on reality? I'm feeling a bit tried at the moment. Perhaps we can continue our conversation when I'm feeling better. What's that? You only have a few more questions? Very well, let's get on with it.

§§§

I see you have your questions written down on a piece of paper. Go on, I'm waiting. Just a minute, I need another cigarette. Now, what is your question? Consciousness is a disease? I'm not following, please elaborate. I once said consciousness is a disease? Once again, gentlemen, you have me confused with that underground fellow. Though I admire him to the point of idle worship, we are not the same. He was a wretched sort who couldn't speak for one minute before contradicting himself. I do agree with him that consciousness is a dreadful thing. Consciousness is where the absurd dwells. To be aware of the world is the beginning of our ontological negation. I'm anticipating your confusion, so be patient. Tell me this: How do we experience the world? You see, Consciousness is the medium which allows us to become self-referential. This most basic of acts, of referencing ourselves in relation to the world, creates the awareness of our finitude. It is at this moment that a split occurs; we are at once in the world and simultaneously removed from it. We have enough consciousness to realize our mortality, but not enough to accept our existential plight. We appear on this plane of existence only to realize we will disappear in a celestial moment. We have the capacity to glimpse the infinite, only to be turned back by the density of despair.

You know, gentlemen, I'm always amazed at how philosophers and theologians tried to resolve the absurdity of our existence. For the religious, escape is found through prayer and contemplation of the divine. For those who are too sophisticated for God; there is artistic expression, political engagement, scientific inquiry, music and a seemingly endless array of human activity. The only problem, of course, is the absurd is never too far behind. It is always lurking, always ready and prepared to strike whenever we least expect it. What does science have to say about consciousness? Science has plenty to say about it, but you may not like it. What we call consciousness is for science nothing more than the sum total of neuro-chemical activity in the brain. How comforting, gentlemen, how so very comforting to hear that we are nothing more than a neuro-chemical petri dish placated by the illusion of autonomous will. Just think of it, gentlemen, billions of cells are chemically interacting with each other in order to produce the illusion that we are more than the sum of our parts. I respect science for telling us the truth about ourselves.

In fact, I praise science for this courageous discovery. Just look at how far we have fallen from God's grace. We went from being the center of the universe to a collection of chemicals that offer us the illusion of being extraordinary. There is nothing remotely special about us. Moving away from the center of the universe was not enough. Look at what happened to us as a result of evolution; we went from the exalted status of being the center of divine creation to being the random outcome of inevitable change. Further insult came when psychology informed us that our thoughts, behaviors, and emotional state is governed by forces that are hidden just beneath the surface of consciousness. Did you know that experts today are telling us that our decisions, choices and actions occur before we are consciously aware of them? I already said that? Said what? Oh, that our consciousness is an illusion that gives us the appearance of being in control? Well, I'm sorry to have repeated myself, gentlemen, but I'm old and don't quite remember the sequence of words I may have said. Now allow me to ask you a question: What are we? Are we nothing more than a chemistry lab? I don't care for the twenty-first century. We are told this will be the century of unprecedented discovery. How many more discoveries do we need before we realize that we are in fact insects. What I wouldn't give to be an insect, gentlemen. At least the insect is not burdened with consciousness that makes it believe it is something more than an insect. More questions?

IX

Very well, go on. What do I think of books? What a curious question, gentlemen? Why do you ask? Technology is changing how we read? No, gentlemen, you are wrong. Technology is killing books. Who needs to read anymore when we are dizzied by an endless supply of images. Say goodbye to your books, gentlemen, they will soon become relics to be housed in museums. We can read online? Have you tried to read the trash they pass off as text? It's maddening! I tried to read online, you know, articles, essays, and so on. I figured I might as well enter the land of the living and become sophisticated like everyone else. I couldn't get very far with all the interruptions. There are these links that you have to navigate and avoid. Reading is like taking a journey through the intellectual and emotional labyrinth of an author. Reading online feels as if the journey is interrupted every few seconds. How can you enjoy the journey if you are constantly prevented from even starting it? Did you know that people don't read anymore? We skim for information. Who has the time to read when we have endless distractions. Social media alone is enough to keep us busy for several lifetimes.

Notes from the Café

I fail to understand the attraction of social media. It is a mass celebration of mediocrity, nothing more. Just look over there, gentlemen. Yes, across from us. Do you see the group of young people sitting? They seem to be together, but they are a world removed. One is talking on her smart phone, and the other two are texting. Don't you love what the twenty-first century has done to language? We've gone from text, which is a proud and noble noun, to texting, a rather grotesquely distorted verb of what the word initially meant to convey. A text used to be a book or essay that signified a certain intellectual sensibility. The very act of texting trivializes and vulgarizes books and ideas. You asked me what I think of books. Well, as you can see for yourselves, books have been replaced with texting. The way people are glued to their phone texting nonstop, you would think they have something profound to say. Alas, gentlemen, texting is nothing but random and inane observations about the absurdity of the everyday. And if texting isn't enough, we now have this new platform... Yes, what is it? Oh, I was just thinking of the word.

The English language is devolving, gentlemen. Wouldn't that make for an excellent book title? The Devolution of Language, what do you think? In any event, there is this social media platform, I'm sure you heard of it, where you can write a few characters at a time. I think it's called shiver or something or other. People seem to think it is the greatest invention since slice bread, but I can assure you it is not. The technology is extraordinary, I grant you that, but what do people use it for? Every mundane minutia of daily life has to be recorded for posterity. If you are sitting twiddling your thumb out of sheer boredom, then you somehow feel compelled to tell the world about it. It is not simply this one website. There are countless other sites and apps that promise us a kind of digital nirvana. We live in the age of instant reality, fleeting images, and ephemeral ideas. We overinflate the value of information and confuse it for knowledge.

Another question? My, but you are a curious lot. You want to know my views on wisdom? It died along with God and philosophy. Who needs old men pretending to have wisdom when you have the omniscient internet permanently attached to your hands? Wisdom today is a click away. Who needs silly old men like us anymore? The twenty-first century is for the youth. Old age has become indecent and vulgar. To live past forty is to defy the moral laws of our enlightened twenty-first century; to live past sixty is an obscene gesture. The old are no longer needed;

no longer wanted and no longer accepted. People like me
are obsolete. We are reminders of an antiquated past and
are politely asked to live in a chicken coop specially
designed for those who are swept under the digital carpet.
Do you know that I once thought wisdom to be the last
remaining human virtue? How naïve I was, gentlemen, how
utterly naïve! There was a time when wisdom was
considered a precious commodity. Those who were
stubborn enough to live past forty were sought after for
their wisdom and sagacity. We lived a true and dignified
life. We were accorded a special place that transcended the
trappings of popular culture.

Alas, gentlemen, today experts and specialists have
taken over. In an intellectual coup of historic proportions,
the experts have succeeded in reducing wisdom to
irrelevant babble. Wisdom was diametrically opposed to
information and, therefore, had to be dealt with. Just as the
digital age was unable to accommodate God, it couldn't
find a place for wisdom. Something had to be done,
gentlemen, something drastic. After all, those who used
reflection to espouse so-called wisdom became a threat to
the new world order. Reflection became a dangerous thing.
Metaphor and personification were anathema to

information and something simply had to be done. It was a contest between analysis and reflection.

§§§

I have it, gentlemen. I just thought of it now. The death of wisdom was the result of an outright linguistic war. A war between those who preferred the efficiency of information and those who continued to cling to the density of language. Information emerged as the winner and to the winner goes the spoils. It's all becoming clear to me now. God was killed off simply because there was no way to linguistically accommodate him. Don't you see, gentlemen? Don't you understand? Religion is based on the language of contemplation and reflection. The information age simply could not find a way to reconcile the simplicity of a metaphor with the endless stream of data that epitomized the twenty-first century. Language evolved to stylistically accommodate myths and stories. What's that? You want me to define information? Well, let me think for a moment. A fair question, gentlemen, you should know I've given considerable thought to it. Information is a set of discrete linguistic packets that distorts and vulgarizes language. When you consider the pace at which we live our lives today, you may begin to understand why language itself is losing its richly textured subtlety. What do you think of my definition, gentlemen? Genius is found in the oddest of places.

You have more questions? Gentlemen, I'm getting tired and I should be going. I want to watch my favorite show on television. Why do you look so shocked? Did I not tell you that I'm a man of contradictions. I am an anomalous accident. I'm the number five. I am living proof that men do not necessarily choose that which is advantageous to them. Go on, what is your question? You want to discuss our temporal nature? What is there to discuss? I remember when time was a companion that never rushed or threatened us. What do you think we the sophisticated ones of today have done to time? We've dissected the hell out of it. We've dissected time like everything else we can get our hand on. We have become a society of punctual neurotics. Everything we do, and I mean every damn thing, is planned and accounted for. We don't experience time so much as we control it. We break it up into temporal packets that are distributed to us throughout the day. We wake up by the clock, work by the clock, spend leisure activity by the clock, sleep by the clock, and in between these activities, we escape the world by going online for a predetermined amount of time.

The irony, of course, is the promise made by the digital age that our lives would be simplified. Don't you just love the term, multitasking? It is the illusion that we have accepted without reservation. Technology allows us to do much more in an ever diminishing time frame. Our lives have become disjointed and fractured. We have compounded our absurdity by keeping ourselves so damn busy that we forgot our contingent nature. We drown ourselves in the materiality of the everyday so that we might not have to be reminded of our irrational foundation. We are always in a hurry; always rushing about, and for what? Rather than embrace our irrational foundation, we are using technology to deny it. The technology we produce, after all, is perfectly rational. There will be a price to pay for the inauthentic games we play. What's that? You have a question about education? I'm actually glad you asked me this question; you might say I'm overjoyed. Do you know what we are doing? We are using education to create more experts and specialist. And those who fail at becoming experts are taught to respect those few who become our new prophets.

Do you know what I call the educated elites of today? I call them half-baked technocrats. That's right, gentlemen, half-baked. This half-baked technocrat is trained to have a great deal of information about a narrow subject matter. Experts are trained to maintain the digital complex we call the twenty-first century. Oh what I wouldn't give to have coffee with an illiterate peasant! The peasant may not be able to read and write, but at least he is authentic. You see, gentlemen, the peasant would use stories and myths to communicate. What does the half-baked technocrat have to offer? I'm sick of this digital age and I'm glad I will depart soon. I'm tired of the irreverent nature of discourse and the false sophistication. I've overstayed my welcome, I grant you that, but I'm glad we had this chat. At least I had the opportunity to say a few final words. What? Why are you looking at me in this peculiar way? The authorities are here? I don't give a damn about them.

What can I do for you officers? You want to know my name? You may call me the Café Dweller. My actual name? I don't know my actual name. Funny, I remember that I once had a name, but it escapes me at the moment. I'm not going anywhere with you. Take your hands off me! Can't you see you are embarrassing me in front of these fine gentlemen? What do you mean you can't see them? They are right in front of you. Why are you arresting me? I've done nothing wrong. Smoking? I can smoke if I want.

Don't touch me! You want me to go with you? I will do no such thing. I'm going home. I had enough stimulation for one day. What do you mean where is home? Don't you think I know where I live? Just give me a minute to remember. This is strange, suddenly I don't remember where I live. What's that? You will take me home? Very well then, I will go with you.

Part II

Apropos of the Midnight Oil

"God is dead. God remains dead. And we have killed him. How shall we comfort ourselves, the murderers of all murderers? What was holiest and mightiest of all that the world has yet owned has bled to death under our knives: who will wipe this blood off us? What water is there for us to clean ourselves? What festivals of atonement, what sacred games shall we have to invent? Is not the greatness of this deed too great for us? Must we ourselves not become gods simply to appear worthy of it?"

__Friedrich Nietzsche

R.F. Georgy

I

What is this place? Where am I? Who are you and how did I get here? Remember? Remember what? Why are you calling me professor? Who are you? If I recognized you, I wouldn't ask for your identity. What is this place? A hospital? I don't belong here. I'm getting the hell out of… Why do you keep asking me if I remember? Remember what? Who the hell are you? David? David Epstein? I don't know a David Epstein. You were concerned about me? What are you talking about? I'm not going to sit down until you tell me what the hell is going on! Very well, I will sit down since you asked politely. Now, David, tell me what is happening. Do I remember you? Look, you are being very mysterious. Please do, I would appreciate some honesty.

Yes, of course, I remember being in the café earlier. What about it? You want to talk about the gentlemen I was with? What do you want to know? their identities? It's none of your damn business. Stop calling me professor! You may call me the Café Dweller. That is my true name and identity. You seem familiar. Have I seen you before? I did? Where do I know you from? We taught together? You taught literature and I was a philosophy professor? That's what the gentlemen in the café told me. Who are... I mean, what are you doing here? If this is a hospital, where did everyone go? What do you mean try to remember? You doubt I was talking to people in the café? Of course I was talking to people in the café. Do you think I conjured them up? Well, think as you well, I feel tired now for some reason. I need to rest. Forgive me, but I can't seem to stay awake. I'm just going to sit here and close my eyes for a few minutes.

I will have plenty of time to rest later? What a curious thing to say. You want to talk about my books? What books? Funny, I was just telling the gentlemen in the café that I was a writer, though I have no memory of writing a single word. You and I engaged in philosophical conversations all the time? You must forgive me, David, but I have no recollection of these conversations you speak of. You want to have a conversation now? I don't think a hospital is the sort of place where you can... Very well, but I need a cigarette. Can we step outside? You know there is a war underway to eliminate us smokers. Are you sure I can smoke inside? Very well, what do you want to talk about? Wait, what is your name again? Oh yes, of course, David Epstein. Are you Jewish? No, no reason, it's just that you look familiar to me. Do you know how much I admire the

Jewish people? Their love of learning alone is awe inspiring.

In any event, what do you want to talk about? For some reason, I feel strange; as if I'm dissolving into nothingness. What an odd sensation. It feels as if the density of my existence is about to unravel into thin air. What's that? Stay focused on you? What do you think I'm trying to do. What? Oh, my books? I told you I have no memory of writing a single book, let alone several. I wrote a novel called Notes from the Café? It sounds familiar. For some reason I have a fondness for cafes. You enjoyed reading it? I'm flattered you read it, if only I can remember writing it. What did you just say? Was I paying homage to Dostoevsky? Now, this is a name I am familiar with. Good old Feyodor! He was an intellectual giant, and yet he was a troubled soul. Do you know that he wrote Notes from the Underground while his wife was dying? He was burdened with debt; a gambling problem, you understand. What joy it brings me that you are interested in such matters. This calls for coffee. I wonder where we can get coffee. You will get us a cup? That's most kind of you.

Funny, I suddenly remember that I indeed authored the novel you speak of. Well, it's more a novella, but what does it matter. I remember! It is indeed strange that my memory suddenly came back to me. In any event, I've always felt that Notes from the Underground was one of the most enduring pieces of literature ever written. The Underground Man was a necessary voice for the nineteenth century. My novel is simply an updated version, something for the twenty-first century. Why did I call it Notes from the Café? I'm not sure now, but I believe it is the result of spending most of my time in a café. I think I actually wrote the entire book in a café, though I can't be certain. I did write the book in a café? How do you know that? You seem to know more about me than what my memory would allow.

§§§

What's that? Do I think I'm the Underground Man? How preposterous you are, David. The Underground Man was a fictional character that Dostoevsky created. You see, Dostoevsky was responding to this fellow, Chernyshevsky, I believe. In any event, this fellow wrote a book about progress and the need to develop a rational foundation for society. I think the book was called, What is to be Done, or something like that. My memory seems to be failing at the moment. Dostoevsky's response was a masterful monologue where he argued that science and reason are incompatible with man's true nature. My character is called the Café Dweller. You might say he is the Underground Man brought back to observe the twenty-first century. You think I took on the persona of the Café Dweller? I did no such thing. You want to know my name? I don't quite remember my name, but I can assure you that I am not the Café Dweller. Ah, coffee at last. Aren't you going to have one? No? Very well, then, Now where was I? I seem to lose my place easily.

Why do you continue to insist that I believe I'm the Café Dweller? I asked you to address me as such? Perhaps I am. I can't make the distinction whether I'm the author or the character. You know who I am, don't you? I can see it in your eyes. Why do you insist that I taught philosophy? Why would I teach a dead subject? Haven't you heard- philosophy is dead. What's that? Why do I engage in philosophical conversations? Philosophy may be dead in the ivory tower, but it still has a place in the café. Did you know that many of the French existentialists wrote much of their philosophical work in cafes? The café is not what it used to be, but I can at least have an intellectual conversation. I was wrong just now; I should have said that a café was, past tense, a place to engage in serious discourse. Alas, cafes today are sterile environments where... Funny, but I feel as if I'm repeating myself. It's as if I don't have full control over my mental faculty.

Why is there no one here? Why do I feel as if I'm in prison? I'm free to go? Well, it was a pleasure, David, but I will take my leave of you now. What do you mean where am I going? I'm going home, of course. Stop this at once. Home is... Well, now you have me. I'm not sure where home is. I'm not sure of anything anymore. Reality seems to be shifting. I feel disjointed and all together disconnected with the world. Can you help me understand what is happening? What's that? I'm the only one that can find my way back to reality? What kind of nonsense is that? Wait, wait just a minute! You do seem familiar. We have met before, haven't we? I remember we used to have coffee together, right? What is the last thing I remember? I remember being in the café when the police arrived.

Do I remember talking about my illness? What illness? Wait, yes I do remember mentioning that I have a rare and incurable disease. Neurocytoma? How do you know that? I suppose I don't have long to live. I was diagnosed last year? You seem to know quite a bit about me. I remember now. I was told I have a few months to live. I'm having that sensation again, as if I'm transparent. I think I want to rest a bit. What's that? You want to talk some more? What do you want to talk about? Why did I leave teaching? I'm not even sure that I ever... wait; it's coming back to me now. I did teach philosophy. I taught for several decades. I think my memory is slowly coming back to me. What does it matter anyway? I'm on my way out and besides, I'm feeling rather tired. I just need to rest for a bit. Would that be alright with you?

You want me to keep talking? But I don't understand. It seems to me you are trying to keep me awake for some reason. What's that? You are offering me a cigarette? This is actually the reason I left teaching. I know it makes no sense, but this is the reason I left. I left teaching because I stopped believing in the rational ordering of human beings. We have become such rationally obsessed creatures that we forgot our irrational nature. I was unable to reconcile my distrust of science and all that was rational with my ability to teach. I felt inauthentic and cheap. I no longer fit into the scheme of things. Everyone was celebrating the digital age and I was becoming a dinosaur. I was becoming obsolete and no one gave a damn. My criticism of the modern world fell on deaf ears. No one wanted to listen to someone writing and lecturing on the folly of progress. You want to know why I find progress so disagreeable? Why am I such an antediluvian? Am I one of those Luddites who rail against technology? Why an avalanche of questions all of the sudden? I'm curious about something. If we taught together for so many years, then you should know why I left. Ah, I see, so you left before me. What's that? Very well, the Luddites.

First, if you recall your history, the term Luddite took on a pejorative meaning that described anyone who had a tough time acclimating to the modern world. The original Luddites were fearful for their jobs as machines inevitably encroached upon their livelihood. Now, if you had read Heidegger's critique of technology, you would be getting closer to my position. The only problem is that I lost all respect for Heidegger once I heard of his complicit role in Nazi Germany. Once he became Rector of the University of Freiburg in 1933, he did everything in his power to remove all Jewish professors. Did you know he had a hand in removing his mentor, Edmund Husserl, who just happened to be Jewish, from his teaching post. I don't care how brilliant he was, he was simply drunk with the promise of power. Would you believe it, he actually had a secret desire to become the philosopher king of the Third Reich. Yes, I mean Plato's version of the philosopher king.

Now, let me tell you… What's that? I truly admire the Jewish people? Of course I do, what did you think? Name for me another people who have suffered so much in history and yet contributed a vast amount of knowledge to our intellectual awareness, can you name anyone who comes close? The Jews are the most genuine people I know. Now what was I saying? Heidegger? Oh yes, of course, A vile man if you ask me. He wrote a small book in 1953, I believe, called the Question Concerning Technology.

His argument was essentially that technology changes our mode of Being. The natural world and everything in it become a means to our technological end. Technology for him was not simply a tool, but a way of Being in the world; a kind of distorted mode of existence. This is where I'm forced to agree with the narcissistic fool. Science and technology have not only changed how we relate to the world, they fundamentally changed who we are. We have been transformed into something inauthentic and grotesquely distorted. Science gives us the illusion of power, nothing more. The gadgets we create only mask the dreadful truth; a truth so painful that we can't bear to confront it. You want to know the truth, don't you? I can see it in your demeanor. The truth is that we will do anything to avoid confronting our existence. We are frightened to death of what we may find. Our consciousness is a private hell. We don't know what to do with it. Technology removes this stubborn fact by helping us escape from our own demons.

II

S cience has liberated us? Listen to me, there is absolutely nothing that is remotely profound in what you just said. Of course, science has liberated us from physical labor, but at what cost? What is the price of these halcyon days we are living in? There was a time when science was running scared from religion. Don't forget that Galileo had to bite his tongue in order to avoid the ultimate punishment. The Church was all powerful then and science was doing much of its work underground. Do you know what I find historically ironic? Science, which was just a fledgling method trying to find its way, accused the church of having too much power. What the hell do you think science is doing today? I'm telling you it has become more powerful now than the church could ever dream of.

If the church promised us heavenly rewards and eternal life removed from the misery of our existence, then science comes along and does one better. It promises us heaven on earth. Do you know what makes this promise extraordinary? It is the ability of science to actually keep its word. The contours of a future heaven on earth are currently being realized in the digital age. Well, I should say the promise of a future hell. Freud was correct, after all, about civilization moving away from God once it was able to better understand the mystery of the world. But Freud was an idiot in not anticipating that science would become our new illusion. If God is a construction, then science is a construction. Every construction needs an army to maintain it and science has its experts and specialists ready to both maintain and move the construction forward.

How odd? Do you hear voices? It is a faint sound, but I hear people talking. I don't know what they are saying. You want me to pay attention to the voices? The voices are becoming more faint. Hmm, they're gone now. What is it you are not telling me? What's that? You know as much as I do? On the contrary, you seem to be guiding this entire discussion along. You still did not tell me who you are? Yes, I know you look familiar, but I can't seem to remember you. Wait a minute. Wait just a damn minute! You're Dave, Dave Epstein. We taught together. It's slowly coming back to me. You taught literature and I was in the philosophy department. We met at café Pamplona everyday around 4pm. I knew you looked familiar. Why couldn't I remember you earlier? I haven't seen you in a long time. What happened to you? You and I used to have epic conversations.

Do you remember the time we discussed the concept of silence for days on end? Do you remember what happened after your book signing? What was the name of your book? Oh yes, I remember now, The Silence in Between. We went to the café and discussed silence until midnight, and after the café closed we went to a diner and talked until four in the morning. We really burned the midnight oil that night. I think the point you were making in your book was that silence exists in the interstitial space of our being. It is good to see you Dave, but where are we? Why did you suddenly leave the university? I never found out what happened to you? Did you get another teaching job? Remember? Remember what? You want me to concentrate on my name? I can't seem to remember. I feel dizzy again. What's that? Freud? I'm tired, Dave. Who the hell cares about Freud. I just want to sleep. For nostalgia's sake? Oh, very well, if you insist, Freud it is.

I do remember our discussions about Freud. I remember you rejected his premise in Future of an Illusion. Me? I actually agreed with him. Freud believed, and rightly so, that as science advances, it would be in a position to answer the worn out interrogatives that were once the exclusive province of religion. Religion would be exposed as an illusion; a kind of childlike projection whose services would no longer be needed. Freud believed that science would liberate us. Hallelujah for science! We can now stand on our own two feet, ready and prepared to answer our own interrogatives. It would only be a matter of time before the cosmic mystery is revealed to us. The future is now, and the illusion has been exposed. God, I miss our conversations Dave! Why did you leave again? You actually had no choice in leaving? What kind of nonsense is this?

What's that? Do I remember my famous rant against science? Which rant? I had many of them. Which one are you thinking of? Oh yes, the one in my lecture. I do remember. I don't know what got into me that day. The students went to see you? I did not know that. They actually told you I was losing my mind? You never told me that story. I never cared for science. It is a little too arrogant for my taste. Here is a line from Hamlet for you that will summarize my point. There are more things in heaven and earth, Horatio, than are dreamt of in your philosophy. Science has become so damn arrogant that it believes it can dissect and explain both heaven and earth. What Freud didn't count on was that science would become our new religion. I know you don't agree, that's why we had endless conversations.

§§§

You believe that Science is an empirical method for investigating the world. What's that? Science does not engage in revealed knowledge? I know that, and I'm sure you will go on to tell me that science does not pretend to have absolute authority over matters that defy observation. That's all fine, Dave, you made this point countless times before. This is what you believe. I know, science is based on verifiable evidence. Science is the only discipline to have a self-correcting mechanism. I grant you all this, but you are missing the fundamental point. I don't care for any system of thought that limits my freedom. I don't care for religion, politics, communism, nationalism, ideology, science, and anything else that uses discursive methods to control and manipulate me. Yes, I actually believe that science is a controlling ideology. Do you remember our discussions of Bertrand Russell?

Of course you remember, what am I talking about? I'm sure you remember his book, Why I'm not a Christian. Do you remember one of his central arguments against religion? He said that religion limits our freedom. Fair enough, but does science not limit our freedom? Have you noticed how science speaks to us? It gives us moral instruction. It tells us how to live. Science does not dispense moral instructions? Of course it does, Dave. Yes, I grant you the method is a noble endeavor, but that's not what I'm talking about. I'm talking about how science is dispensed to the rest of us. Humor me for a minute, who the hell gave science the unilateral authority to tell me what to do? Science does not possess any authority? That's a laugh! Dave, you must be losing your mind.

What about thou shalt not smoke, thou shalt exercise, thou shalt seek therapy, and so on? It's for our benefit? That's a laugh! Do I need to remind you that using discursive language is power? This reminds you of our discussion of Foucault and Kuhn? It should, we've had countless discussions concerning both. Both rejected science as ideological? True, but I don't agree with them on this point. When you have knowledge supported by endless data and research, it takes on canonical authority. Science is an ideology in terms of how it is dispensed to the rest of us. Do you want to hear something interesting? When I was diagnosed with my rare disorder, my doctor told me that I should immediately quit smoking. I asked him under whose authority should I stop. He looked at me as if I was crazy and responded with contempt by telling me, actually yelling at me, that I should quit smoking if I know what's best for me.

What's that? We cannot expect science to explain the research behind every study? Ah, now we are getting somewhere. So you are saying that it is easier to simply tell people the outcome of all the studies by using moral language to communicate the outcome? Yes, of course, I see your point. I mean, how else would you inform everyone? Do you know that's the same argument the church made centuries ago. They offered people moral advice. They asked people to trust them; that theology is a complex subject matter and the church knows what it's doing. Don't you see? Don't you understand? Both religion and science use the same language of control and manipulation. I'm sure you want to say that science is an enlightening agent whose interest is only to find answers and solutions. You would be correct, of course, science is interested in finding answers, but its arrogance makes you believe that it has all the answers. Do you know what Russell said about science?

He said something to the effect that what science cannot explain, mankind cannot know. Now do you understand what I'm trying to tell you? Science has become

the absolute ruler of both heaven and earth. Who needs
God when you have science taking over the world with
spectacular results? Do you know what the difference is
between Moses and a man holding a smart phone? You
don't know? Well, just humor me. You don't know what to
say? The difference is that Moses needed divine
intervention to manipulate reality. The man with a smart
phone can manipulate reality with the touch of a screen.
When science can achieve efficacy by the simple touch of a
screen, it becomes far more powerful than all religions
combined. Nietzsche suspected as much when he declared
God dead some one hundred and fifty years ago. He
realized that progress and belief in the divine were
incompatible. The only problem is that Nietzsche declared
God dead a little too early.

What do I mean? Nietzsche didn't make a
distinction between the God of philosophy and the God of
the masses. The God of philosophy was effectively dead by
the time Nietzsche made his famous declaration. It's sad to
see God reduced to an irrelevant footnote. There was a
time when God stood proudly atop the syllogistic
mountain, but philosophers wouldn't leave well enough
alone. Descartes, who was religious, reduced God to an
insurance agent who guaranteed his existence. Come on,

Dave, we had this discussion countless times before. I need another cigarette. Here are the voices again. I can't make out what they are saying. Something very strange is going on here. You want to hear more about Descartes? Very well, then, when Descartes was trying to establish an epistemological framework, he decided to engage in what he called methodical doubt. He doubted everything, including the physical world, his own existence and even the validity of mathematical knowledge.

Once he established his existence, you know, the famous Cogito Ergo Sum, he proceeded to bring back the physical world. The problem, of course, was how can he guarantee that his mind was not playing tricks on him. Enter God. Descartes' entire philosophy requires God to guarantee that he exists and, for that matter, everything else he believes in also exists. God is the guarantor of his clear and distinct ideas, remember. Now, let's look at what happened to philosophy since Descartes. Wait, The voices are getting louder now? Can't you hear the voices, Dave? What is happening? I'm feeling so tired. Can we continue this discussion another time? It feels like we're burning the midnight oil once again. You miss those days? What's that? Very well, I will continue for a little while longer since you insist.

III

Let me finish my thought on the philosophical death of God. From Descartes we go to David Hume who rejects God as incompatible with evil in the world. Once Hume was done wreaking havoc on metaphysics, others would follow to remove God from the conversation. Feuerbach and Marx argued that God is a necessary construction needed to keep people in a subaltern state of quiescence. Freud made a similar argument as we already discussed. By the time we get to the French existentialists, God was no longer considered a topic worthy of discussion. This is what happened to the philosophical God, he died a most ignominious death. The God of the everyday man continued to live on, weakened perhaps, but still alive. Philosophy was just a prelude to what was to come. Are you with me so far?

You agree with me that God became a problem for philosophy? Well, I'm glad you are coming around. what's that? Ah, you doubt that science had anything to do with God. Of course you are going to say that, Dave. I'm sure you will also tell me that science neither affirms nor denies the existence of God? You would like to know if I believe in God? What a strange question? You and I have discussed God countless times and you know my position. You want to know if my position has changed? Why would it change? You know that I believe in God. I believe in God out of spite. That's right, don't look so surprised. Out of spite for science, I will believe in God. You see, the modern world presents me with two options: believe in a construction that has been thoroughly debunked and exposed as a fantastic fairytale, or submit to the cold indifference of science. I choose the comfort of the construction. I choose to believe in a fairytale rather than be fooled by the seductive logic of science.

Yes, I said construction, what about it? Ah, now we get to the heart of the matter. You want to know if I accept the existence of a supreme being, right? Dave, you know that I do accept that God exists. I accept it despite every effort of my intellect telling me not to believe. I accept God because I am more than the sum total of my intellectual parts. What's that about Pascal's wager? No, I don't need his wager to embrace the divine. To me God represents everything that I am not. God is a non-contingent, absolute being who holds the mystery of my finitude. I am a sick man, Dave, and when you are sick you tend to want to embrace something, anything that transcends your fragile nature. As I approach the end of my life, I wonder what was all the intellect used for. I have read hundreds of books, written a few, though I can't remember them, and what has knowledge done for me?

Think about it, Dave, here I am living out the final moments of an absurd life and all the philosophy in the world couldn't get me an inch closer to the truth. Is there any difference between someone standing on the shoulders of intellectual giants and an illiterate peasant? What the peasant lacks in sophistication he makes up in wisdom. Knowledge is a tenuous thing, you understand. It is always messy, uncertain of its direction, and pompous. Do you know that Western civilization has been obsessed with rational evidence, and for what? Do you remember when we stayed up until four in the morning discussing Berger's idea of signals of transcendence? We never met the man, but do you remember how shocked we were when we read his book, A Rumor of Angels? Given that he was a sociologist, we naturally assumed he was an atheist, remember? I mean, he wrote such books as An Invitation to Sociology, The Social Construction of Reality, and so on. When did we read A Rumor of Angels? Oh yes, it was in the late sixties.

§§§

Do you remember the point he was trying to make? Yes I know it was a long time ago, but for some reason, I remember his book as if I read it yesterday. I liked the fact that Berger didn't look upon metaphysical proofs as if they were the highest authority governing our beliefs. Berger preferred something simpler and existentially appealing. He simply looked for signals of transcendence in the trivial and mundane reality of the everyday. In a way, Berger was searching for God's fingerprints rather than demand his identification. We, and when I say we I mean Western history, have gone about establishing a connection with the divine by demanding proof. Proofs are a tricky thing, you see. I mean, can we prove that we exist? There are many beliefs that we cannot prove in this world, yet we embrace them. What's that about evidence?

Yes, I do believe that evidence, as you put it, is irrelevant. What about you, Dave, are you telling me that you require evidence before you can believe? Don't tell me, extraordinary claims require extraordinary evidence, right? I don't think you've carefully examined what you are saying. You make it sound as if there is a cause-effect relationship between evidence and belief. It's as if evidence is the sine qua non of belief. Let me ask you a question: Have you ever fallen in love? We had this discussion before? Well, humor me for a minute. Let's suppose you tell me you are in love with your wife and my response is that I demand proof of your affirmation. What would you offer me? If you had to prove your love for someone, how would you do it? I mean what is love? Is it an emotional state? Could it simply be a chemical concoction in the brain? You know, love is an interesting human experience. It is the one irrational behavior we can get away with. You don't know what I'm getting at?

I'm talking about proof, damn it! What do we mean by proof? Have you given it any thought? Ah, anything that is verifiable and reproducible, very good. So you accept Russell's arrogant notion that if science can't prove something, it is unknowable. You believe the only true and credible knowledge comes from science. But science gives us probabilistic answers, isn't that right? You believe in probability. What a waste of intellect, don't you think? Do you believe in anything absolutely? You do? Such as? Tell me, what is it that you believe absolutely? Very well, you believe in love and family. Why should you? There is no verifiable evidence that can prove to me your sincerity. How can anyone be certain that you love your family? Your family is certain of your love? Yes, I'm sure they are, but tell me; can someone believe in God without bothering with proof? Why can't that be sufficient?

You don't believe in God, do you, Dave? You require proof in order to embrace fairytales. What would you do if scientific proof was offered to you on a silver platter? Would you get on your hands and knees and ask the almighty for forgiveness? You are absolutely right, Dave, science can't investigate metaphysical claims. So what you are saying is that you require scientific proof in order to believe in God, but science is incapable of investigating such nonsense. How do you like your circular reasoning so far? Excellent, you are an agnostic. I'm sure you take comfort in such a position. Agnosticism is not messy or offending. You are neutral when it comes to God. You hold out for the possibility, but will reject any proof that does not come from science. How convenient it must be to request the kind of proof that science cannot provide, while simultaneously rejecting any other form of knowledge as meaningless babble.

What's that? I speak as if I actually believe in God? I just told you that I believe in a supreme being. What? Believing in God out of spite is not actually believing in

God? Now we get to the heart of the matter. You don't accept that I believe in God, do you, Dave? Perhaps you know me more than I know myself, but I do believe that we all have an impulse towards transcendence. I believe our intellect is often our worst enemy. We interrogate the dense opaqueness of the universe only to be slapped by the absurdity of silence. We believe that the universe cares about our trivial cries for answers. I am not contradicting myself. I grant you that I have contradicted myself more times than I care to remember, but not this time. To believe in a transcendent reality is to believe in something that goes beyond the universe, immense as it is. I believe in God because my intellect is useless. Your agnosticism hides behind an intellect that believes it has the ability to discern a valid proof if and when it is offered.

What's that, Dave? I don't care for the modern world? If you I recall, you never cared much for it either. Do you remember our discussion about Huxley and Orwell? Yes, we spent a few weeks discussing them. You do remember? I remember that I couldn't bring myself to agree with either of them. They both painted a dystopian future, but I don't think they fully captured the modern world. Yes, I remember agreeing with Huxley about the triviality of a culture that celebrates mediocrity as the benchmark of happiness. You, of course, didn't see it that way. What was your argument, Dave? Oh yes, I remember now. You felt that technology has helped educate millions of people, which is infinitely better than the illiterate peasants of old. This is where you are wrong, my friend. Technology has reengineered us to become slaves to its will.

Both Orwell and Huxley believed the value of our lives would be diminished in the future. In 1984, Orwell painted a totalitarian future where texts and ideas are banned. In Brave New World, Huxley imagined a world where technology drowns us in a sea of trivial information. Yes, I did agree with Huxley on this point, but, if you remember, I also agreed with Orwell on a totalitarian future. You don't remember me agreeing with Orwell? Well, let me refresh your memory, Dave. Orwell's future was supposed to be an all-powerful political structure that controls our every thought and action. What ended up happening is that an all-powerful technological structure is now in control of our thoughts and actions. We have today created the most subtle form of control and manipulation ever devised by man.

I'm describing Huxley? Not quite. You see, Huxley imagined a future organized and run by a benevolent dictatorship that programs us to accept our enslavement. I don't think the digital age works this way. The digital age is far more abstract and diffuse than we realize. Science is a construction that presents itself as transparent and reproducible. It offers us stunning results and unheard of miracles. But… do you know what I find most striking about science? There is a certain banality about what it can do. In its repeated capacity to magically manipulate the world, science has become comfortable and familiar, like an old shoe that we can't bring ourselves to toss aside. Science now rules with absolute authority. There is no benevolent dictatorship to rule over us. Science is rendering all dictatorships irrelevant. This is what I find so damn frustrating about science, Dave.

We perceive the world through a scientific lens. We may not understand how science works, but we are all willing to be its disciples. We no longer believe in a heaven that is transcendent and removed from the reality of the everyday. Why should we? We have science promising us heavenly rewards in the here and now. We no longer need God to intervene on our behalf; we have technology to answer our prayers. We no longer… what's that? I'm in lecture mode? I suppose I am. I'm ascribing too much power to science? No, Dave, this is where you're wrong. I don't think I'm ascribing enough power. You see, what makes science the most powerful cultural force in human history is its ability to influence us by making us believe that we are in control of our lives. As the most powerful epistemology ever devised by man, science is now in a position to rule over the intellectual landscape unchallenged. Philosophy is dead because there is nothing else to contemplate.

Science has no room for contemplation. You know what I find tragic, Dave? It is not so much that we no longer contemplate, but that we no longer know how to contemplate. We are so damn busy chasing information that we forgot how to relax over a cup of coffee. Do you know what I realized now, Dave? After centuries of political, economic, religious, and ideological control, the most powerful and effective method of keeping man busy twiddling his thumb is to distract him. We are so busy playing with our shiny machines that we no longer bother with philosophical questions, let alone think for ourselves. We have become narcisstic idiots drowning in a sea of information. Technology has cannibalized language and left us only the skeletal remains. That's all we really need to text and tweet.

What happened to us, Dave? Have you seen people text? They do it with such urgency and alacrity that you would think they are conveying something profound.

Alas, they are only interested in the mundane distractions of the everyday. People have become living zombies. This is what Huxley feared and, in this regard, he was absolutely correct. What's that? I'm ignoring all the benefits that science and technology offer us? Are you kidding me, Dave? Science doesn't need me to praise its bloated accomplishments. For every scientific or technological achievement there have been a thousand intellectual setbacks. What did you say? Man's nature? Hmm, I was going to say that man is stupid by nature, but that would be an exaggeration, albeit a slight one. The philosophical answer has always been an either/or proposition; man is either good or evil by nature.

§§§

I think we are all frightened creatures who engage in endless distractions in order to avoid confronting our consciousness. We are always searching for ways to amuse ourselves in order to distract us from the brutal reality of what it means to exist. This is why science has succeeded in spectacular fashion. It offers us endless distractions. The twentieth century has conquered our physical limitations. Machines eliminated our need to use physical strength to manipulate the world. This created a new category of human experience. A whole industry was needed to accommodate the empty leisure hours. To pass the time we created entertainment to amuse ourselves. The digital revolution, as they call it now, is on the verge of conquering our mental limitations. Now, let me ask you this, Dave, what happens to us when machines take care of our physical and mental needs? What becomes of us? Some optimists believe we will be able to tap into our creative nature and become the next Mozart.

What rubbish! What? You think that's possible? Rubbish! Do you know what man will do with his extra time? He will find more ingenious ways to escape himself. He will invent virtual worlds to make himself feel useful. What technology has done is mask our restless nature. We have become so addicted to the shiny toys that science throws at us that we have forgotten how to live in our own skin. Imagine what would happen if all the technology that governs our lives stopped for one day. What do you think will happen? We will scream in existential agony. Our true nature, naked and exposed, will rear its ugly head and the absurd will laugh with utter delight. What's that? I'm going too far in my critique? Perhaps I am, Dave, but what has science done to change my mind?

Do you know that people likes us are dinosaurs? There is a war underway to get rid of us intellectuals. We are tolerated only in so far as we keep our criticism confined to the ivory tower. Those who hail the benefits of the digital age are embraced as visionaries and the rest of us are marginalized as antiquated fools who do not possess the requisite sensibility to appreciate the modern world. Plato and Aristotle are no longer wanted. Ideas are a dangerous thing, you understand. Who the hell needs a metaphor when you have information? Why bother thinking or coming up with an original thought at all? We have created the illusion that progress is all we need. We have become overly comfortable and complacent with our smart phone and tablets. We believe that if we busy ourselves with the endless details of our technological lives that we are contributing something to the world. You see it differently? Of course, you see it differently. You've always held out hope that science will overcome the challenges of our discontent.

Do I remember the debate? Which debate are you referring to? Oh the one where you and I were invited to be on a panel discussion? I remember I was outnumbered. How many people were on the panel? It must have been seven or eight. What's that? There were only four? Well, it felt like more. I was the only one who lashed out against the digital age. What's so funny, Dave? The audience tuned me out? Of course, they tuned me out. It was as if I was speaking a foreign language. No one wants a Kafkaesque diatribe against modernity. I told you, we accept the ready-made reality that is offered to us. Did I ever tell you why I've always admired Dostoevsky? He was a man who saw through the false sophistication of the nineteenth century. He truly understood the dangers of a world governed by rational principles. I don't care for a world that reduces us to mathematical principles. Remember, Dave, twice two isn't always a four. I know you are going to suggest that we are capable of being a four.

V

I know what you are going to… wait, I hear the voices again. what is this place? Why was I brought here? Why is there no one else here? You keep telling me to remember. What is it you want me to remember? I'm a patient here? What is this place? Who the hell are you? Don't I know what? What is going on, Dave? I am trying to remember, damn it! Oh dear God in heaven! You died several years ago. I remember. I remember! I gave the eulogy at your funeral. How am I having a conversation with you? Am I dead as well? That would explain this nightmare I'm having. What is this laughter I hear? Dave, are you there? Dave! Who is there laughing? Who are you? You're the absurd? What kind of nonsense is this?

What do you mean I created you? You are a voice in my mind? So you are a chemically induced hallucination, which makes you, and everything else I experienced recently, an illusion. What's that? I might be an illusion as well? That's preposterous! I'm the one who is in control of my own thoughts. Cogito, ergo sum, remember. Descartes was wrong? None of this is real? Well, of course none of this is real, but I am certain of one thing: I'm alive and I'm in control of my own thoughts. If you are a hallucination

I'm having, at least I can choose which hallucination I want
to interact with. To hell with you, of course I can choose.
Choice is an illusion? Who said that? I did? Where did
Dave go? I know I manufactured him, but I enjoyed our
conversation. Who the hell are you? You are the evil genie?
Of course I remember Descartes' evil genie, but… I don't
understand.

I thought you said you are the absurd. You are a
projection of my inner demons? What demons? Why can't
I see you? You are just a voice in my mind? What's that?
I'm in hell? There is no such thing as hell so leave me in
peace. I'm leaving this God forsaken place. How do I
propose to do that? Watch me. What do you mean there is
no leaving this place? Hell has no exit doors? There is no
such thing as hell. Yes I know I said I believe in God, but I
don't believe in a hell. If you are me, then why are you
laughing? I don't find this situation amusing in the least.
You are laughing at the absurdity of it all? Why are you
convinced this is hell? Well, you might be convinced, but
I'm not. Yes, I remember Sartre declaring that hell is other
people. Sartre, of course, never believed in God so hell for
him was the crushing density of others. I hear voices again.
I'm getting out of here. What do you mean there is
nowhere to go? I'm going towards the voices. That's what I

should've done in the first place. To hell with all these illusions in my mind. I must be in some kind of extended dream. I must find a way to hear what they are saying.

"Hello doctor. The family had a few questions for you, but they left. I was about to text you to let you know they will return tomorrow. I'm sorry you had to drive down this late."

"That's alright. I'm actually here to look at his latest CT scan. Did they bring them up?"

"Yes, they brought them over an hour ago. Let me get them for you."

"No need. I'm sure they uploaded them. Let me check them on my phone. Have you noticed any change from last week?"

"No change at all, Although, his BP was elevated when I checked an hour ago. His wife and children have been visiting every day. My sister, you know the one who is studying literature, gave me one of his books to read."

"Which book?"

Notes from the Café

"Notes from the Café. I read four or five chapters, but I didn't care for it. He seems to be a bitter man."

"He's actually a brilliant man. I met him once when I attended a talk he gave at Harvard. He dissected the modern world in a way that I was forced to question some of my beliefs about science."

"Well, he doesn't seem brilliant to me. I couldn't understand what he was saying. He's lashing out at the world."

"It would help to read Dostoevsky's Notes from the Underground. His book is an updated version of the Underground Man."

"Well, I'm not as well read as you, doctor."

"His scan just loaded. Let me see now. Hmm, it doesn't look good. I will have to consult with Dr. Fletcher, but I think he had a second stroke."

"Do you think he can pull through?"
"It doesn't look likely. His cancer has metastasized. I think you better call his family. He might not make it through the night."

"Poor fellow! You know when I was an undergrad, I had to write a paper on one of his books. I didn't care for his ideas then. Years later, I picked up Notes from the Café and it had an enormous impact on me. I suppose he will live on in his books. You know what I learned from him? Every age needs an Underground Man to remind us that science can't solve all our problems."

"Do you think he can hear us?

"You never know with coma patients."

§§§

What the hell! of course I can hear you. I'm here! Can you hear me! Dave! Where are you? So this is what existence entails. It makes perfect sense to me now. We do everything in our power to escape our consciousness. We immerse ourselves in the world in order to not confront the irreducible I. What is consciousness but an acute sense of the unknowable and impenetrable I? The absurd is the illusion created by chemicals that fool us into believing we are special and unique. In the end we are nothing but a mystery created by probability. We are thrown-in-the-world only to be condemned to struggle for some clue as to why. We are lead to believe that we want meaning, but what we really want to do is twiddle our thumbs in restless anticipation. We are forever restless, down to our last breath. We are freaks of the universe. We are intimately part of creation and simultaneously strangers who never truly belong.

I am now confronted with my own death, but I can't find meaning in the eternal negation of what I once was. I remember reading Heidegger's Being and Time and... what was that line I found particularly profound? What the hell am I without my memory? Yes, I got it. Dasein is an entity where within its own Being lies Being as an issue of serious contemplation. I remember reading this as an undergraduate and thinking what kind of doublespeak is this. I once existed in the world, engaged in the-world and here I am, but for a brief moment, pure mind. I am in a position to contemplate my existence unencumbered by the layers of identity that accumulates over a lifetime. I no longer have access to the world, but I have access to Being; my Being. I am curious about my consciousness, wherein my stubborn ontological essence lies. What will I find as I peel away the ontological layers of a mystery that is impenetrable? The opacity of my consciousness is preventing me from gaining any insights.

Heidegger was wrong. It took me a lifetime to know that. There is no way to shed light upon consciousness when the very object you are shedding light upon is the object in question. How does one get at the ghost in the machine? My machine has failed me and all I am now is a ghost who just might be an illusion created by chemical synapses gasping for their last breath. I get it now. I get it now! There is no essence to shed light upon. There is a linguistic barrier to my ontological mystery. We chase the circles of language hoping to gain some insight into something we can' t possibly understand. Philosophy wants to offer us logically consistent answers that appeal to our intellect. Science wants to dissect us like worms by promising us empirical evidence. I am acutely aware of my thoughts, but I can't seem to get at the ontology that is generating these thoughts. My memory is all but gone now, but I still have the capacity to think.

what is it about death that frightens me? Is it because I'm going to miss people? That would be silly. How can I miss anyone if my identity will be erased for all time? What is it, then? Perhaps I'm afraid of the permanence of death; the absolute finality of it all. There is something profoundly absurd about coming unto existence for a fleeting moment in time and then returning to the mystery that was. Why exist at all? People often say the gift of life. What the hell kind of gift was it? No one asked me if I want to exist. I must be slipping away. My thinking is becoming less lucid. How the hell can someone ask me if I want to exist? In order to be asked, I would have had to be conscious. The only way to come unto existence is without my permission. There isn't anything I can do about it now. I seem to be a passive observer of the inevitable. I may not ever fully grasp the meaning behind my existence, but I'm beginning to realize something about death.

Death is the negation of every category of human understanding. It is the negation of every human emotion. It is the negation of love and hate, happiness and joy, thoughts and memory, pain and suffering, hopes and dreams, and every other category created by the illusion of consciousness. How can belief in anything help me now? The living are talking about me as if I'm already gone and the dead have returned to the void. I'm standing at the threshold of nothingness and it is terrifying. One minute I'm filled with disjointed memories that summarize a life, and the next I may disintegrate into a permanent void. Philosophy and religion may talk all they want about death and dying, but it is only an intellectual exercise. I exist now only as consciousness, trapped under the illusion that I somehow matter in the grand scheme of things. I can't even remember who my wife and children are. I suppose if I concentrate, I might remember them, but I feel weak now.

What do I do? Think, damn it! I was a writer, professor of philosophy, a husband, a father, and several other identities that are about to fade into oblivion. Heidegger wanted us to peel away the layers of identity to get at some level of truth, but what truth? What did all my learning do for me? What is man but a collection of identities stored as feeble memories? If you remove the identities, what do you have left? I am pure mind now, left to contemplate the absurd in my naked isolation. Sartre was wrong, he had it all wrong. Hell is not other people. Hell is to be left alone to dwell upon a consciousness that reveals nothing. The living can escape the absurd and the dead have no need for it. I'm slipping further away now. I can hardly form a thought. Everything is fading. What is happening? My voice is fading. Is this what happens when we die? The voice, my voice, fades into nothingness? At last, the dying of the light. I am but a footnote to the absurdity that was. Rest at last.

R.F. Georgy was born in Cairo, Egypt. After studying philosophy at the University of California, Berkeley, Georgy devoted himself to writing. His articles have appeared in the Los Angeles Times, Christian Science Monitor, Daily News Egypt, as well as several other outlets. His novel, Absolution: A Palestinian Israeli Love Story, will be published later this year. He is currently writing a novel on Nietzsche's Parable of the Madman.

R.F. Georgy

9 780615 986050